USBORNE WORLD HISTORY
THE LAST 500 YEARS

Jane Bingham, Fiona Chandler and Sam Taplin

Designed by
Susie McCaffrey and Linda Penny

Consultants: Gary Mills and Dr. Anne Millard
Illustrated by Giacinto Gaudenzi, Inklink Firenze and Ian Jackson
Map illustrations by Jeremy Gower
Managing editor: Jane Chisholm
Managing designer: Mary Cartwright

Contents

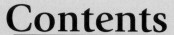

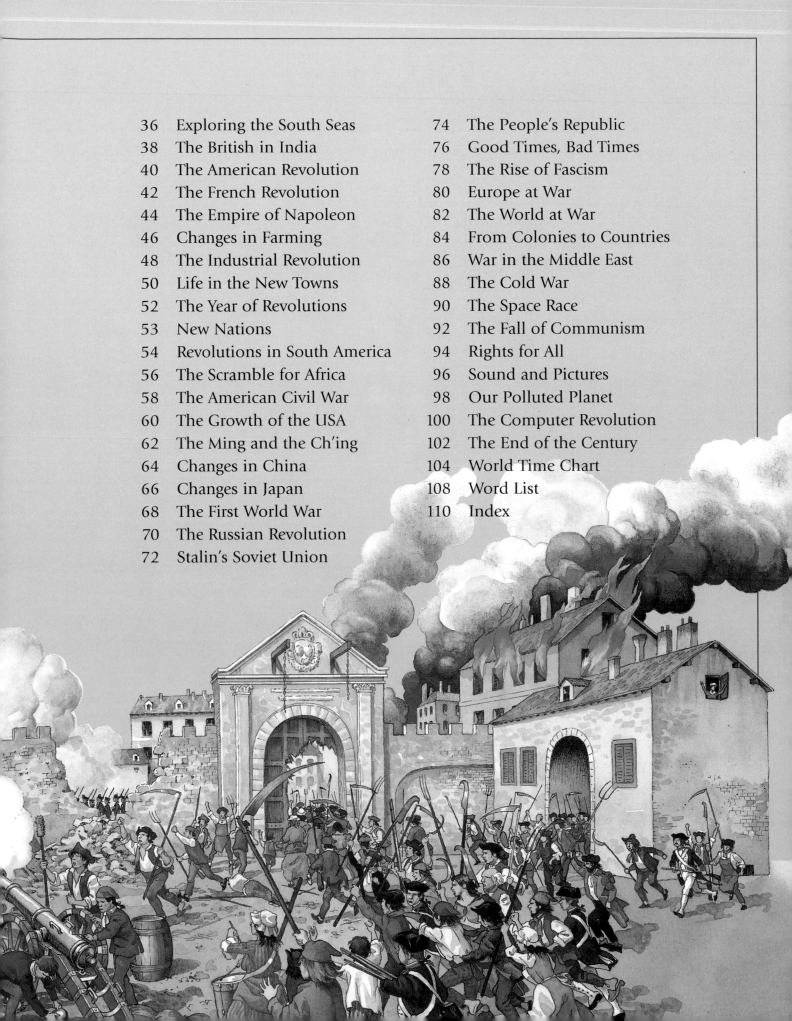

Looking at the Last 500 Years

Between the years 1500 and 2000, life changed dramatically in most parts of the world. At first, this transformation happened gradually, but by the 1800s people's lives were changing fast, and in the 20th century things really gathered speed.

Changing journeys

Moving from place to place in the 1500s was very slow and difficult, and journeys didn't get much easier for 300 years. Travel started to change in 1804, when the first steam train was built. Around 80 years later, the motor car was invented, and by the 1960s planes could cross the globe in hours, and spacecraft had taken astronauts to the Moon. By the end of the century, unmanned spacecraft had reached most of the planets in our solar system.

The American Henry Ford made motor cars that lots of people could afford. Here he is in one of his cars, around 1920.

Fighting for freedom

During the 16th century, a few powerful rulers governed large areas of the world, and ordinary people had very little say in how their countries were run. This began to change in the 1700s, when new ideas of rights for all spread through Europe and America. Rebels struggled to gain more freedom, and gradually more and more people won the right to vote for their country's leaders. Today, people are still fighting for freedom in many parts of the world.

This is a scene from the time of the French Revolution in 1789. It shows a man setting off to join the revolutionaries.

Science and technology

Daily life in the 1500s was extremely hard, but over the next 500 years new discoveries and inventions slowly changed people's lives. Advances in medicine meant that people lived much longer, while new machines made everyday tasks faster and easier. In the 20th century, cars, computers and television transformed the way that many people lived.

This is the Hubble Space Telescope. It allows scientists to see farther into space than they ever have before.

World views

Most people in 1500 had no idea what the world looked like and many still believed that the Earth was flat. Gradually, over the next 500 years, scientists and explorers built up a picture of the globe. Today, satellites can take photographs of the Earth from space, and people can see television pictures of places all over the world.

Where did it happen?

There are maps throughout the book to show you exactly where things happened. You can also check which area of the world you are reading about by looking at the bottom corner of each page. The different areas of the world are shown on the map below.

NORTH AMERICA
EUROPE
ASIA
MIDDLE EAST
SOUTH ASIA
FAR EAST
AFRICA
SOUTH AMERICA
AUSTRALASIA

This is the diary of Anne Frank, a young Jewish girl who described her life in hiding during the Second World War.

How do we know?

Historians study history by collecting lots of different kinds of evidence. They piece this evidence together to create a picture of what happened in the past.

Letters and diaries give first-hand accounts of things that happened in the past, newspapers contain the news and views of the time, and government records provide many useful facts and figures. Maps give a clear idea of which parts of the world were known and explored, while scientific papers and notebooks describe experiments and discoveries.

Since the 1860s, photography has provided a vivid record of events all over the world. Historians who study the 20th century use film and sound recordings to help with their research, and also interview people about their memories and experiences.

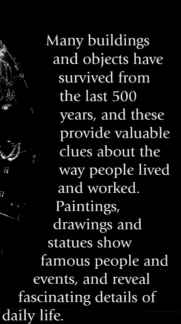

Many buildings and objects have survived from the last 500 years, and these provide valuable clues about the way people lived and worked. Paintings, drawings and statues show famous people and events, and reveal fascinating details of daily life.

Many historians have studied film showing the murder of the US President John F. Kennedy in 1963. Here you can see the President and his wife minutes before he was shot.

Exploring the World

The 16th century was a very exciting time for explorers. After Christopher Columbus arrived in America in 1492, people dreamed of finding treasure in the exotic New World. They also hoped they would find new routes to the rich trading countries of China and India.

Around the world

The Portuguese explorer Ferdinand Magellan discovered a route around South America into the Pacific Ocean. Magellan died during the voyage, but one of his captains, Sebastian del Cano, continued sailing west until he reached Europe. This was the first voyage around the world and it proved that the Earth was round.

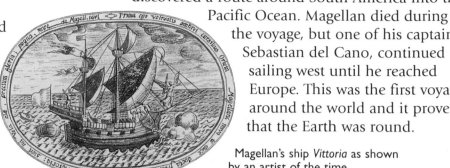

Magellan's ship *Vittoria* as shown by an artist of the time

Spices and jewels from India

Exploring Canada

Jacques Cartier, a French explorer, sailed along the east coast of what is now Canada, searching for a new route to China. Later, he canoed up the Saint Lawrence River, and reached a small village which he named Montreal.

Sailing northwest

An English expedition led by Martin Frobisher tried to reach China by sailing around the top of Canada. Frobisher believed he had found a way around Canada, but in fact he had only sailed into a bay.

Sailing northeast

A Dutch sea captain named Willem Barents hoped to find a route to India by sailing northeast past Norway. His ship became trapped in ice in the Arctic Ocean, but he managed to build a shelter, and stayed there until the ice melted.

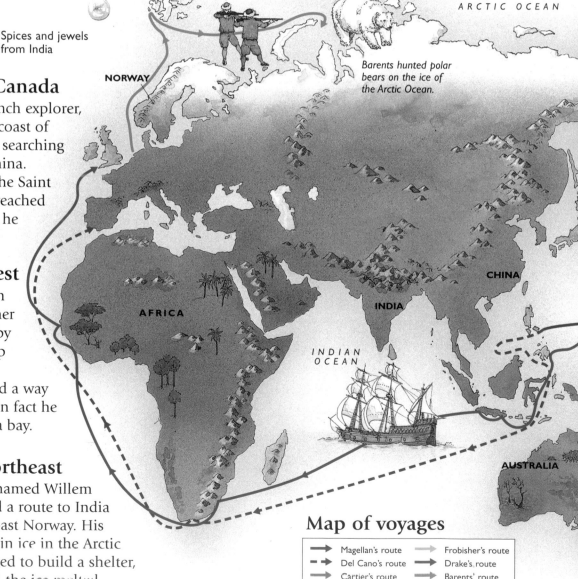

ARCTIC OCEAN

Barents hunted polar bears on the ice of the Arctic Ocean.

NORWAY

AFRICA

CHINA

INDIA

INDIAN OCEAN

AUSTRALIA

Map of voyages

→ Magellan's route	→ Frobisher's route
⇢ Del Cano's route	→ Drake's route
→ Cartier's route	→ Barents' route

Spanish conquerors

Spanish soldiers, known as conquistadors, arrived in Central and South America, determined to win land and gold. They defeated the Aztec and Inca people who lived there, and destroyed their powerful empires.

A gold Aztec ornament

Along the Amazon

A Spanish explorer, Francisco de Orellana, sailed along the entire length of the Amazon River in South America. His boat was often in danger from fast-flowing currents.

Sailing and stealing

Sir Francis Drake of England was a skilled sailor and a daring pirate. He sailed all the way around the world, stealing treasure from Spanish ships as he went.

A miniature portrait of Sir Francis Drake

CANADA

Cartier explored Canada with native North Americans as his guides.

Montreal

PACIFIC OCEAN

ATLANTIC OCEAN

CENTRAL AMERICA

Explorers brought back pineapples from Central and South America.

Amazon

SOUTH AMERICA

Important dates

1519-1521	Spanish conquistadors conquer the Aztecs.
1519-1522	Magellan's ship sails around the world.
1532-1534	Spanish conquistadors conquer the Incas.
1534-1536	Cartier explores eastern Canada.
1542	Orellana sails along the Amazon.
1576	Frobisher reaches northern Canada.
1577-1580	Drake sails around the world.
1596	Barents reaches the Arctic Ocean.

THE WORLD

The Ottoman Empire

The Ottomans were Muslim Turks who were governed by a powerful ruler called a sultan. By 1500, they had built up a large and well-organized empire with its capital in the magnificent city of Istanbul.

The empire grows

During the 16th century, the Ottomans gained land in the Middle East, North Africa, Russia and Hungary. In 1529, they threatened western Europe by attacking Vienna, but eventually a Christian army drove them out of the city.

Struggle for sea power

By the 1550s, the Ottoman navy had gained control of the Mediterranean Sea. This frightened the rulers of Spain and Italy, and in 1571 they fought the Ottomans in the sea battle of Lepanto, near the Greek coast. The Ottomans lost the battle, but they soon won back control of most of the Mediterranean.

The Ottomans built many beautiful mosques. This is the Blue Mosque in Istanbul, where the Ottoman ruler Sultan Suleiman is buried.

Strong sultans

The Ottoman sultans lived a life of luxury in the Topkapi Palace in Istanbul. The most powerful sultan was Suleiman, a great ruler and warrior, who became known in Europe as Suleiman the Magnificent.

Sultan Suleiman

Using Christians

The Ottomans captured boys from Christian areas of the empire and brought them up as Muslim slaves. Many of the slaves were trained as soldiers, called janissaries, but the most intelligent ones became officials in the empire. The slaves were very useful to the sultans, because they were completely obedient to their Ottoman masters.

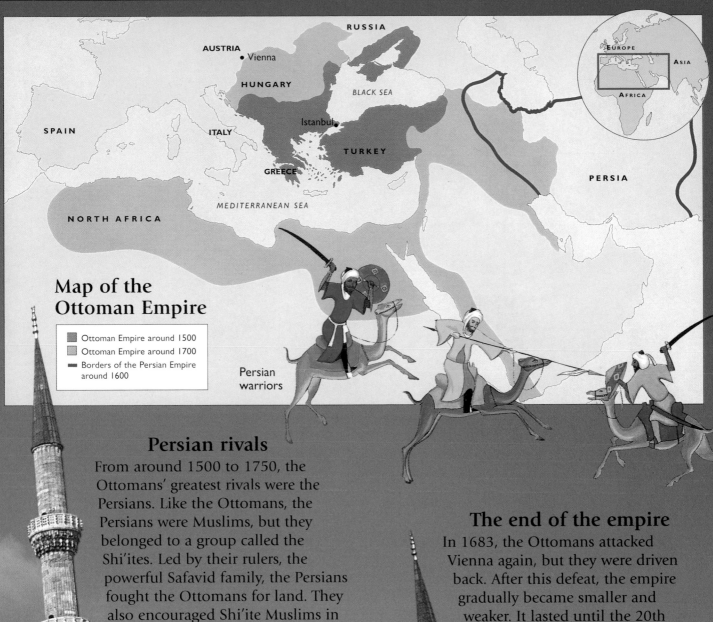

Map of the Ottoman Empire

- Ottoman Empire around 1500
- Ottoman Empire around 1700
- Borders of the Persian Empire around 1600

Persian warriors

Persian rivals

From around 1500 to 1750, the Ottomans' greatest rivals were the Persians. Like the Ottomans, the Persians were Muslims, but they belonged to a group called the Shi'ites. Led by their rulers, the powerful Safavid family, the Persians fought the Ottomans for land. They also encouraged Shi'ite Muslims in the Ottoman Empire to rebel.

The empire weakens

After 1600, the Ottoman Empire continued to grow, but it was ruled by a series of weak sultans who couldn't control their people. At the same time, some of the sultans' enemies, such as Russia and Austria, grew stronger.

The end of the empire

In 1683, the Ottomans attacked Vienna again, but they were driven back. After this defeat, the empire gradually became smaller and weaker. It lasted until the 20th century, but by the end of World War I it had collapsed completely.

Important dates

1520-1566	Sultan Suleiman rules the Ottomans.
1529	The Ottomans attack Vienna.
1571	The Battle of Lepanto
1683	The Ottomans attack Vienna for the last time.
1918	The Ottoman Empire comes to an end.

THE MIDDLE EAST

The Mogul Empire

The Moguls were Muslims from the area now called Afghanistan. Like their ancestors, the Mongols, the Moguls were great warriors, but they also loved poetry and art, and created beautiful gardens.

The first emperor

In 1526, a Mogul prince named Babar led his army into India. He defeated the Sultan (ruler) of Delhi at the Battle of Panipat and took control of northern India, becoming the first Mogul Emperor.

Akbar the Great

Babar's grandson, Akbar, won large areas of land from the Hindu princes who ruled most of India, but he still managed to keep the Hindus loyal to him. He did this by marrying a Hindu princess, and by allowing the Hindus to worship their own gods and goddesses. Akbar ruled for almost 40 years. He ran his empire very efficiently, and invited painters, poets and scholars to his splendid court at Agra.

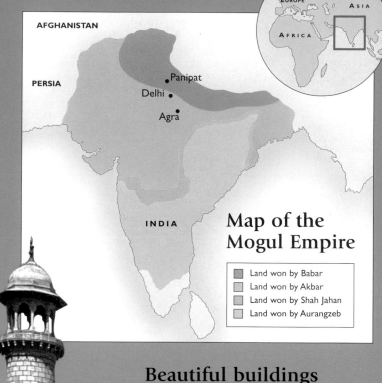

Map of the Mogul Empire

- Land won by Babar
- Land won by Akbar
- Land won by Shah Jahan
- Land won by Aurangzeb

Beautiful buildings

The Moguls built amazing mosques, forts and palaces, but their most famous building is the Taj Mahal, near Agra. It was built by Akbar's grandson, Shah Jahan.

Emperor Shah Jahan built the Taj Mahal as a tomb for his beloved wife, Mumtaz Mahal.

A Mogul painting showing the marriage of Emperor Akbar's brother

SOUTH ASIA

A cruel emperor

The Mogul Empire reached its greatest size under Shah Jahan's son, Aurangzeb. But Aurangzeb was a cruel man and an unpopular ruler. In order to become emperor, he put his father in prison and murdered his two older brothers. Once he had gained power, Aurangzeb forced the Indian peasants to pay very high taxes. He also destroyed many Hindu temples and built mosques on top of their ruins.

The Taj Mahal is built from white marble and took 11 years to complete.

Armies and traders

After Aurangzeb's death in 1707, there were no more strong emperors. A Persian army invaded northwest India, and the Hindu princes slowly won back land from the Moguls. Meanwhile, traders from Europe began to set up trading stations all over India.

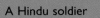

A Hindu soldier

The end of the Moguls

By 1750, the Mogul emperors were losing control of their empire. India became divided into small states ruled by princes, and the European traders grew more and more powerful. Gradually, the British East India Company took over the running of India, and the Mogul emperors lost all their power (see pages 38 and 39).

Important dates

1526	Babar wins the Battle of Panipat.
1526-1530	Babar is the first Mogul Emperor.
1556-1605	Akbar is emperor.
1628-1658	Shah Jahan is emperor.
1658-1707	Aurangzeb is emperor.
1714	The Hindu princes start to win land.
1737-1739	The Persians invade northwest India.
1857	The last Mogul Emperor gives up his throne.

Catholics and Protestants

By the 1500s, many people were unhappy with the Catholic Church. They thought that its leaders were only interested in wealth and power, and complained that many of its priests were badly educated and lazy.

A few determined people protested about the Church. At first, they tried to reform or improve it, but later they broke away completely. Their followers became known as Protestants, and the movement they started was called the Reformation.

Martin Luther, the leader of a growing protest against the Catholic Church

Luther's protest

In 1517, a German monk named Martin Luther wrote a list of 95 ways that the Catholic Church could be reformed. He nailed the list to the church door in Wittenberg, and his ideas soon spread. This made the Church leaders furious, and in 1520 the Pope issued a document that banished Luther from the Catholic Church for ever.

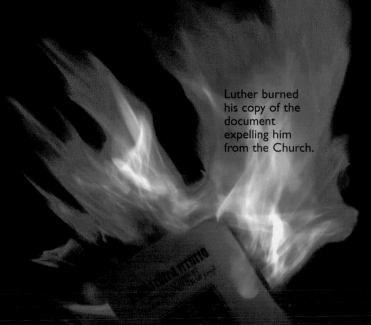

Luther burned his copy of the document expelling him from the Church.

Luther's changes

Luther went into hiding and worked on his ideas for how the Church should be run. He believed that church services should be kept simple, and that people should read the Bible for themselves, instead of learning everything from priests. Luther translated the Bible from Latin into German, and many copies of his Bible were printed.

By 1525, people all over Germany were holding simple services based on Luther's ideas, and the Lutheran Church was born.

John Calvin

In 1541, John Calvin, a French reformer, started the Calvinist Church in Geneva. Calvinism is a strict form of Protestantism, and it was very popular in Switzerland and Scotland. By 1560, large numbers of people in northern Europe had become either Lutherans or Calvinists (see map).

John Calvin, founder of the Calvinist Church

Henry's rebellion

King Henry VIII of England argued with the Pope because he refused to allow Henry to divorce his wife, Catherine of Aragon. In 1531, Henry decided to take the place of the Pope, and made himself head of the Church in England, which later became known as the Anglican Church.

Henry VIII thought many monks and nuns did not lead holy lives, so he closed down the abbeys where they lived. Most of these abbeys are now in ruins, like Rievaulx Abbey shown here.

EUROPE

Catholics fight back

The leaders of the Catholic Church tried hard to win people back to their Church. They made many changes, which together became known as the Counter-Reformation.

During the Counter-Reformation, sculptors carved beautiful statues for Catholic cathedrals and churches. This statue of St. Teresa and an angel is by the Italian sculptor Bernini.

The map shows the different Christian groups in 1560.
- ☐ Mainly Catholic
- ☐ Mainly Lutheran (Protestant)
- ☐ Mainly Calvinist (Protestant)
- ☐ Mainly Anglican (Protestant)
- ☐ Mixed Catholic and Protestant

Map of Europe

Catholic leaders set up colleges for priests, built elaborate churches, and trained teacher-priests, called Jesuits. They attacked the Protestants in sermons and books, and also used the Inquisition, a system of courts run by monks, to find and punish Protestants.

Religious wars

During the 16th century, Protestants and Catholics fought each other all over Europe. One of the bloodiest struggles took place in France where French Protestants, known as Huguenots, fought the Catholic king and his supporters. The most horrific event in the French wars was the St. Bartholomew's Day Massacre, when thousands of Huguenots were slaughtered by Catholics. Eventually, after 30 years of war, the Huguenots were given the freedom to worship.

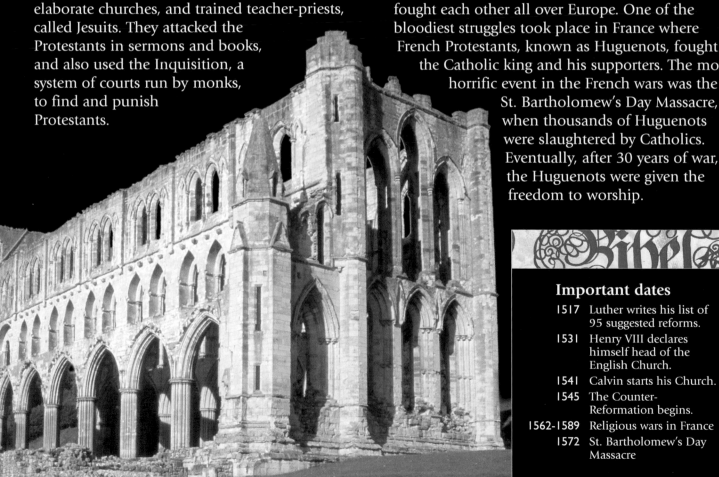

Important dates

1517	Luther writes his list of 95 suggested reforms.
1531	Henry VIII declares himself head of the English Church.
1541	Calvin starts his Church.
1545	The Counter-Reformation begins.
1562-1589	Religious wars in France
1572	St. Bartholomew's Day Massacre

EUROPE

Elizabethan England

Elizabeth I was the last and greatest of the Tudors, a line of kings and queens who had ruled England since 1485. She reigned for 45 years, making England a rich and powerful country that was respected throughout the world.

Great entertainment

Elizabethan England was famous for its writers and composers. The queen invited poets and musicians to entertain her at court, concerts were held in nobles' houses, and plays were performed in new London playhouses, such as the Globe Theatre.

In this portrait, Elizabeth I wears thick, white face paint and a dress that is covered with jewels.

Mr. WILLIAM
SHAKESPEARES
COMEDIES,
HISTORIES, &
TRAGEDIES.
Published according to the True Originall Copies.

This is the title page from a collection of plays by William Shakespeare, the most brilliant of all the Elizabethan writers.

Elizabeth's people

Although lots of merchants became rich in Elizabeth's reign, many of her people were still very poor, and some had to beg in order to survive. In 1563, the first Poor Law was passed. This allowed local officials to raise money to look after the poor.

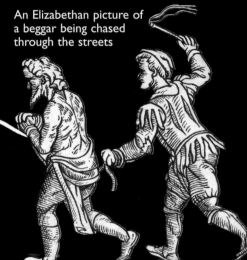

An Elizabethan picture of a beggar being chased through the streets

Catholic plots

Elizabeth was a Protestant, but some people wanted a Catholic ruler instead. A group of English Catholics tried to replace Elizabeth with her Catholic cousin Mary, Queen of Scots, but all their plots failed.

Explorers and raiders

During Elizabeth's reign, the great explorer Sir Francis Drake sailed around the world (see page 7), and Sir Walter Raleigh started a colony in North America. But English captains like Drake and Raleigh were raiders as well as explorers. They attacked Spanish ports and stole treasure from Spanish ships.

EUROPE

The Spanish Armada

King Philip II of Spain was furious that the English were raiding Spanish ships, and he decided to lead a Catholic attack on England. In 1588, he sent a large fleet of ships, called an armada, to invade England. The Spanish ships sailed to the Netherlands, where an army was waiting to join them, but on their way through the English Channel they were attacked by English warships.

Frightening fire ships

After four fierce sea battles, the Spanish fleet anchored close to Calais, on the northern coast of France. During the night, the English surprised the Spanish by sending eight fire ships (ships that had been deliberately set on fire) into the middle of the fleet. The Spanish panicked, and their ships scattered in all directions.

In this scene, English fire ships are approaching the Spanish Armada.

The fire ships are packed with rags, timber and oil.

The end of the Armada

The morning after the fire ships attacked, the English and the Spanish fought the sea battle of Gravelines. The battle lasted all day, and the Spanish were defeated.

After the battle, the Armada's ships were blown north. The Spanish were forced to sail around Scotland and Ireland, and most of their ships were wrecked in terrible storms.

Map of western Europe

- Lands ruled by Spain
- → Route taken by the Armada

EUROPE
ASIA
AFRICA
SCOTLAND
IRELAND
NETHERLANDS
ENGLAND
Calais
FRANCE
SPAIN
NORTH AFRICA

The fire ships are carried toward the Armada by the wind and the tide.

As the fire ships approach, the Spanish sailors panic and cut their anchor ropes.

The Spanish are terrified by fire because their ships are carrying gunpowder which might explode.

Heat from the flames makes the ships' guns fire.

Important dates

1558-1603	Elizabeth I is queen.
1563	The first Poor Law is passed.
1564-1616	Life of William Shakespeare
1577-1580	Sir Francis Drake sails around the world.
1588	The Spanish Armada is defeated.

EUROPE

15

Kings, Cavaliers and Roundheads

In 1603, James I became King of England and started a new line of Stuart rulers. James I and his son, Charles I, believed that God had chosen them to be supreme rulers and so they refused to accept any control from Parliament. This led to violent arguments.

The Civil War

In 1629, after several clashes with Parliament, King Charles I decided to rule without its help. Charles ruled alone for 11 years, but eventually he was forced to ask Parliament for money. Parliament refused to help, and in 1642 fighting broke out between the king's supporters and Parliament. This struggle is known as the English Civil War.

Followers of the king were called Royalists or Cavaliers, and supporters of Parliament were known as Parliamentarians or Roundheads. Some Cavaliers had flowing hair and fancy clothes, while most of the Roundheads were Puritans (very strict Protestants), who disapproved of fine clothes, acting and dancing.

The New Model Army

At first, the Cavaliers won most of the battles in the Civil War, but then a Puritan named Oliver Cromwell decided to reorganize the Roundheads' troops.

A 17th-century portrait of Oliver Cromwell

Cromwell's new fighting force was called the New Model Army. In 1645, it won the Battle of Naseby, and the following year the king was forced to surrender.

King Charles I, painted by the artist Van Dyck

Killing the king

For two years, there was no more fighting, but then war broke out again. Eventually, Parliament gave up any hope of agreeing with the king, and in 1649 Charles I had his head chopped off in front of a stunned crowd in London.

The dramatic death of Charles I, as shown by an artist of the time

Commonwealth and Cromwell

After Charles' death, Parliament ruled England for four years. This period of time was known as the Commonwealth. But Parliament did not govern well, and in 1653 Oliver Cromwell took control of the country, calling himself Lord Protector of England. Cromwell ruled efficiently but strictly. He closed down many ale-houses and declared that Christmas Day was no longer a holiday.

King Charles II

When Cromwell died, many people wanted to have a king again. The son of Charles I had escaped to France, and he was welcomed back and crowned King Charles II. The return of Charles II is called the Restoration.

Charles II, a popular king who loved music, dancing and beautiful women

Plague and fire

During Charles II's reign, a dreadful disease, known as the plague, killed thousands of people in London. The following year, a terrifying fire swept through the city. The fire destroyed hundreds of buildings, but it also killed the rats that spread the plague.

The Great Fire of London raged through the city for four days. In this scene, the flames have reached London Bridge.

Rebuilding London

After the fire, large areas of London were rebuilt, using stone instead of wood. The architect Sir Christopher Wren designed over 50 churches for the city, and by the 1690s London had many elegant new buildings. People strolled through public gardens, and merchants met in coffee houses to make deals with each other.

This is St. Paul's Cathedral in London, Sir Christopher Wren's most famous building.

A strong wind helps the fire to spread quickly.

London Bridge has many wooden houses on it and they burn very easily.

People try to cross the Thames to safety.

Important dates

1603-1625	James I is king.
1625-1649	Charles I is king.
1642-1648	The English Civil War
1649-1653	Parliament rules England (the Commonwealth).
1653-1658	Oliver Cromwell is Lord Protector of England.
1660-1685	Charles II is king.
1665	The Great Plague of London
1666	The Great Fire of London

EUROPE

17

The Power of the Habsburgs

The ambitious Habsburg family began ruling Austria in the late 13th century. By marrying into some of Europe's richest families, they gained vast areas of land, and soon became the most powerful rulers in Europe.

The empire of Charles V

In the first half of the 16th century, the Habsburg emperor Charles V governed large areas of Europe, as well as colonies in the Americas. Charles was a strong ruler who defended his empire well. He won wars against the French and drove an army of Ottoman Turks out of Vienna (see page 8).

The empire divides

In 1556, Charles V retired to a monastery, dividing his lands between his son, Philip II, and his brother, Ferdinand. Philip II became King of Spain, and also controlled Italy, the Netherlands and Spain's American colonies, while Ferdinand ruled from Austria and inherited the title of emperor.

Map of Europe

☐ Empire of Charles V

SWEDEN
DENMARK
ENGLAND
Magdeburg
BOHEMIA
NETHERLANDS
Vienna
HUNGARY
AUSTRIA
FRANCE
SPAIN
ITALY
AFRICA

This is King Philip II of Spain, who became fabulously wealthy when Spanish settlers in America started mining gold and silver.

The Thirty Years' War

The Thirty Years' War started as a religious struggle between Protestants and Catholics in central Europe. It began in Bohemia (now part of the Czech Republic), when a group of Protestant nobles threw some officials of the Catholic Habsburg emperor out of a window.

This 17th-century drawing shows the event which helped to start the Thirty Years' War.

Spain and the Catholic German states supported the Habsburg emperor, while Bohemia was joined by Denmark and the Protestant German states. Later, Sweden and France also fought against the Habsburgs. By the end of the Thirty Years' War, the Habsburgs had become much less powerful.

The War of the Spanish Succession

The last of the Spanish Habsburgs was Charles II, who died in 1700. Charles had no children, so he left his lands to his distant relative, Philip, the grandson of the French king. The English and the Dutch were afraid that France and Spain would unite, so in 1701 they formed a "Grand Alliance" to fight against France.

The war lasted for 13 years and many European countries joined in. Eventually, the Alliance allowed Philip to become King of Spain, on the understanding that France and Spain would always remain separate. This was the end of the Habsburgs in Spain, but they still ruled in Austria.

Maria Theresa

In 1740, the 23-year-old Maria Theresa became the new ruler of the Habsburg Empire. When she took over, the empire was poor and weak, but she managed to make it strong again. Maria Theresa welcomed many musicians and artists to her court in Vienna. One of these musicians was the brilliant composer Wolfgang Amadeus Mozart.

This portrait shows Maria Theresa, who ruled the Austrian Habsburg Empire for 40 years.

Here you can see the Schönbrunn Palace in Vienna, which was rebuilt by Maria Theresa.

The later Habsburgs

During the 18th and 19th centuries, the Habsburgs lost more and more land. But they managed to stay in power until 1918, when the last Habsburg emperor gave up his throne.

Important dates

1519-1556	Charles V rules a vast Habsburg Empire.
1556	The Habsburg Empire is divided in two.
1618-1648	The Thirty Years' War
1701-1714	The War of the Spanish Succession
1740-1780	Maria Theresa rules the Habsburg Empire.
1918	The last Habsburg emperor gives up his throne.

EUROPE

The Rise of the Dutch

By the 1550s, the low-lying lands that are now Holland, Belgium and Luxembourg were divided into 17 areas, called provinces. The people of the provinces had grown rich by weaving cloth and trading, but they weren't independent. Instead, they were ruled from Spain by the powerful Habsburg family (see page 18).

Catholics and Protestants

In 1556, King Philip II of Spain became the new Habsburg ruler of the provinces. Many people in the provinces were Protestants, but Philip was determined that they should all be Catholics. He sent the Duke of Alba to punish any rebels, and when two Protestant leaders were executed, war broke out between the provinces and Spain.

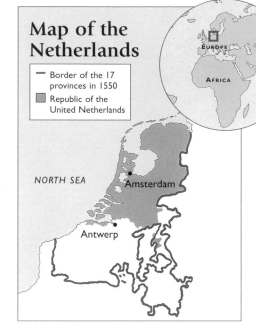

Map of the Netherlands

— Border of the 17 provinces in 1550

▨ Republic of the United Netherlands

EUROPE
ASIA
AFRICA

NORTH SEA

Amsterdam

Antwerp

The Dutch Revolt

Led by a Dutch prince named William of Orange, the people of the provinces fought fiercely for their independence. This struggle is known as the Dutch Revolt, because the most determined fighters were the Dutch, who lived in the northern provinces.

A miniature painting of Prince William of Orange

Dutch independence

In 1581, the seven northern provinces declared that they were independent from Spain. They called themselves the Republic of the United Netherlands and chose Prince William of Orange as their ruler.

In 1648, Spain finally accepted that the Republic was independent. This was the start of a new country called the Netherlands, which is now also known as Holland.

The city of Amsterdam

During the Dutch Revolt, the wealthy port of Antwerp was destroyed by Spanish troops, and many of the provinces' merchants and bankers moved north to Amsterdam. The city of Amsterdam was rebuilt around a network of canals, and by the 1600s it was the busiest port in Europe.

This picture shows the bustling port of Amsterdam.

Merchant ships from all over Europe visit Amsterdam.

French trading ship

Art and science

This painting is by Jan Vermeer, who was famous for his scenes of everyday life.

During the 17th century, many great artists, thinkers and scientists lived and worked in the Netherlands. Inventors made microscopes, telescopes and clocks, and artists painted portraits and scenes of daily life.

The Dutch Empire

The Dutch built up an efficient navy and set up trading bases in Asia, South Africa, America, and even Japan. But their most valuable bases were in the East Indies (present-day Indonesia and Malaysia). From there, Dutch merchants sent shiploads of precious spices to Europe.

Using the land

The flat fields of Holland were often flooded by sea water, but Dutch engineers discovered new ways of draining the land. Some farmers made a fortune by growing exotic flowers from Turkey, known as tulips.

Dutch tulip-growers developed a wide range of flowers. Here are three kinds of tulips, painted by a 17th-century artist.

One tulip bulb could cost as much as a large country house.

William and Mary

In 1677, Prince William of Orange, great-grandson of the first Dutch leader, married the English princess Mary, and in 1689 they were crowned joint rulers of England. William ruled the Netherlands and England until his death in 1702, but the Dutch lost control of England when Mary's sister Anne became the next English queen.

This Dutch merchant ship is bringing spices from the East Indies to the Netherlands.

Important dates

1568 The Dutch Revolt begins.

1581 The Republic of the United Netherlands is created.

1648 The Republic of the United Netherlands is recognized by Spain.

1689-1702 William of Orange is ruler of the Netherlands and King of England.

EUROPE

21

France and the Sun King

King Louis XIV of France, known as the Sun King, was the most powerful ruler in 17th-century Europe. He controlled all of France for over 50 years, without ever consulting his nobles or the French parliament.

Louis XIV became known as the Sun King after he played the role of the Sun in a 12-hour ballet. This golden carving shows Louis as the Sun King.

Early lessons

Louis was only five when he became king, so his mother ruled for him. But after five years, the people of Paris rebelled, angry at the high taxes that they had to pay. Many nobles joined in the revolt, and Louis was forced to leave Paris.

In 1653, the rebellion collapsed, but Louis was still too young to rule on his own, so a powerful Church leader, Jules Mazarin, governed France on his behalf. Louis finally took control in 1661 when he was 22. He was determined that there would be no more revolts, so he kept all the power for himself, becoming what is known as an "absolute" ruler.

Running France

To help him run the country, Louis chose advisers who were talented, but loyal to him. His chief adviser, Jean Colbert, reorganized laws and taxes, set up new businesses in France and increased trade with other countries. Colbert also built new roads, canals and bridges all over France.

The Palace of Versailles

Louis gave orders for a magnificent palace to be built at Versailles, near Paris. Over 30,000 workers were needed to build the palace, which was filled with priceless statues, tapestries and paintings. In 1682, Louis moved to Versailles with his family and thousands of servants. He also forced many French nobles to live in the palace, so that he could keep an eye on them all the time.

Here you can see Louis XIV's palace at Versailles. Its extravagant Baroque style was copied all over Europe.

The palace gardens were laid out in a very formal design.

This is the glittering Hall of Mirrors in Louis's palace at Versailles.

Wars in Europe

Louis wanted to conquer more land, and he fought many wars against other countries in Europe. The wars made France feared and respected, but they were very expensive and the French gained only small areas of new land.

Anger in France

In 1685, Louis took away the French Protestants' right to worship, and many of them fled abroad. Meanwhile, the French middle classes and peasants began to resent the taxes that they had to pay to keep the king and the nobles in luxury.

A splendid court

Louis XIV's court at Versailles was famous for its drama, music and art. The playwright Molière wrote comedies to amuse the king, the musician Lully composed operas for the court, and artists painted flattering portraits of the king and his family.

This dramatic portrait of Louis XIV shows him as a dashing young horseman.

After the Sun King

The two French kings who ruled after Louis XIV were both very extravagant. Like the Sun King, they fought expensive wars and lived in incredible luxury.

Meanwhile, the French people continued to pay heavy taxes, and 70 years after the Sun King's death, the French Revolution began (see pages 42 and 43).

Important dates

1643-1715	Louis XIV is King of France.
1643-1651	Louis's mother rules for him.
1648-1653	Rebellion in Paris
1661	Louis XIV takes control of France.
1667-1713	France fights wars against other countries in Europe.

The Age of Ideas

Between 1600 and 1800, there was an explosion of new ideas in Europe. Scientists made dramatic discoveries, thinkers questioned the power of their rulers, and some daring writers challenged the teachings of the Church. Many people started to see the world in a new light, and the 18th century became known as the Age of Enlightenment.

Discoveries in science

By observing the world around them and doing experiments, scientists made amazing progress. Johannes Kepler studied the way planets move, and Galileo Galilei used the newly invented telescope to help him prove that the Earth circles the Sun. Robert Boyle experimented with chemicals and gases, and Isaac Newton discovered how gravity works.

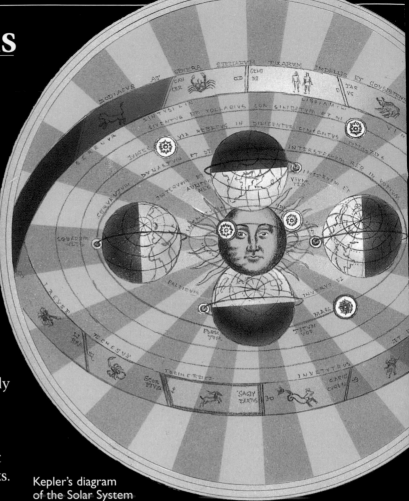

Kepler's diagram of the Solar System shows how the planets travel around the Sun.

The photograph on the left shows the surface of the Moon. Galileo studied the mountains of the Moon with the help of a telescope.

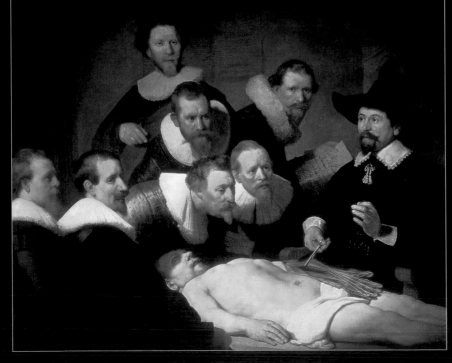

Advances in medicine

During the 17th and 18th centuries, doctors studied the human body, and surgeons performed difficult operations. Many doctors were forced to study secretly because the leaders of the Church wouldn't allow them to cut up dead bodies.

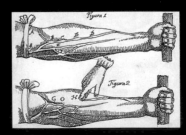

In 1628, William Harvey described the way blood moves around the human body. This is a diagram from Harvey's book.

This painting by the Dutch artist Rembrandt shows a group of 17th-century doctors examining the arm of a dead man.

Collecting knowledge

Many books were produced to record the new discoveries that were being made. Denis Diderot put together a 35-volume encyclopedia. Dr. Samuel Johnson wrote a vast English dictionary, and Carl Linnaeus published detailed studies of plants, dividing them into types, or species.

Linnaeus gave each plant a Latin name. The pansy shown here was named *Viola tricolor*.

Spreading ideas

The new ideas spread fast among educated people. Discoveries were published in books, pamphlets and newspapers, and scientists formed societies where they shared their findings.

Rich people invited guests to their homes to discuss the latest discoveries, and people also met in coffee houses to read the newspapers and talk about ideas.

Scientists often used models to help them explain their ideas. This is an 18th-century model of the Sun and the planets.

Rulers and ideas

Some European rulers encouraged the search for knowledge. King Louis XIV of France set up a society which paid scientists to carry out experiments, while Charles II of England started the Royal Society for scientists and thinkers. Charles also built an observatory, where astronomers could study the stars.

Dangerous ideas

By the 1750s, thinkers in Europe had become very daring. In France, Jean Jacques Rousseau made the bold new claim that all people are equal, while Voltaire attacked the French king and the Church. Ideas like these got their writers into trouble, and Voltaire was sent to prison three times.

Like Voltaire and Rousseau, the writer Thomas Paine encouraged ordinary people to think about their rights. His most famous book, *The Rights of Man*, supports the ideas behind the French Revolution.

The writing in this 18th-century cartoon suggests that Thomas Paine's ideas were dangerous nonsense.

This golden ball represents the Sun.

These smaller balls represent the planets, which all move around the Sun.

Some planets have moons circling them.

The model works when its handle is turned.

Important dates

1620s	Kepler studies the movement of the planets.
1630s	Galileo proves that the Earth travels around the Sun.
1660s	Newton discovers the laws of gravity.
1694-1778	Life of Voltaire
1712-1778	Life of Rousseau
1791-1792	Thomas Paine writes *The Rights of Man*.

Changes in Russia

Russia in the 1500s was a fast-growing country ruled by a powerful tsar, or emperor. But Russia's position on the eastern edge of Europe made it isolated from the wealthy west. Large areas of Russia were too cold to grow food, and most Russians were peasants who were desperately poor.

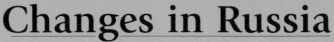

This is a portrait of Ivan the Terrible, a powerful ruler who was often violent and cruel.

Ivan the Terrible

In 1547, Prince Ivan IV of Moscow became Tsar of Russia. He was a strong ruler who encouraged trade with western Europe, built up the Russian army, and won land in the valley of the Volga river.

At home in Russia, Ivan was ruthless and cruel, earning himself the title of Ivan the Terrible. He seized land from Russian nobles, called boyars, and gave it to his personal followers. He also made a law that took away all the peasants' rights, turning them into serfs who couldn't leave their master's land.

St. Basil's Cathedral in Moscow was built by Ivan the Terrible to celebrate his victories in the Volga valley.

The time of troubles

The chaotic period that followed the reign of Ivan the Terrible is known as the "time of troubles". During this time, several men claimed that they were the true tsar, and the country was divided by civil war. Meanwhile, Russia was attacked by Sweden and Poland. However, the Russians did manage to win more land, in the vast eastern area known as Siberia.

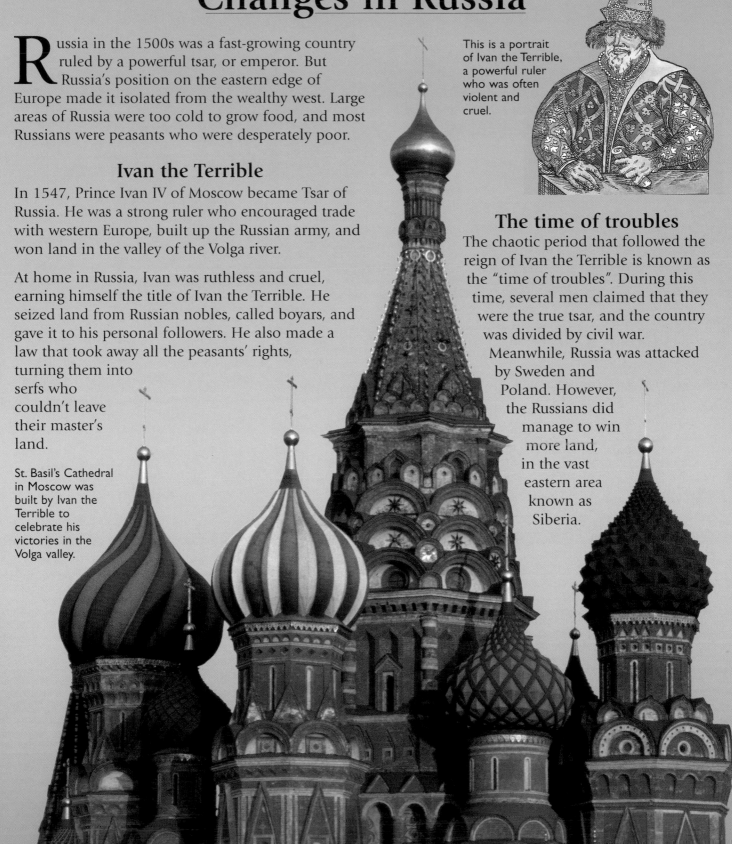

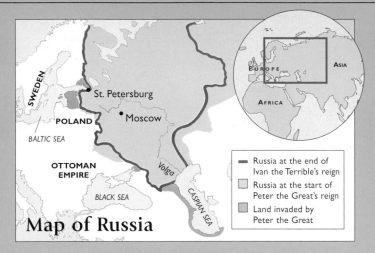

Map of Russia

Legend:
- Russia at the end of Ivan the Terrible's reign
- Russia at the start of Peter the Great's reign
- Land invaded by Peter the Great

Peter the Great

In 1613, the Romanov family took control of Russia, starting a dynasty which would last for 300 years. The greatest of the Romanovs was Peter the Great, who became tsar in 1689. By the end of his 36-year rule, Russia was one of the strongest countries in Europe.

Learning from the west

Peter decided to modernize Russia by copying the way western countries were run. He spent 18 months in northern Europe, visiting factories, farms and hospitals, and he even worked in a shipyard.

Peter the Great was an energetic and inspiring leader, but he could also be frighteningly brutal.

Changing Russia

Back in Russia, Peter reorganized his country's government, and reduced the power of the boyars. Workers from Europe helped to build canals, ships and factories, and a new iron industry was set up in Russia.

Peter forced the boyars to cut off their beards, to show that they had given up their old powers. This cartoon shows him as a barber.

Peter's wars

Peter strengthened the Russian army, created a navy, and won several victories against the Swedes and the Ottoman Turks. From Sweden, Russia gained a stretch of land beside the Baltic Sea. This meant that the Russians could at last build some ports which were close to western Europe and didn't freeze solid every winter.

A new capital city

Peter gave orders for an elegant new city to be built on the Baltic coast. He named it St. Petersburg and made it into Russia's new capital. The land around St. Petersburg was extremely swampy, and hundreds of serfs drowned while they were building the city.

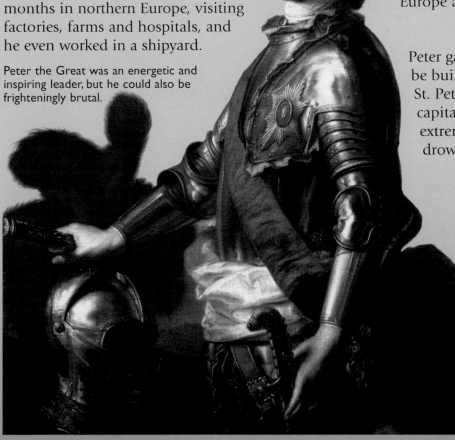

Important dates

1480-1505	Prince Ivan III of Moscow is the first Tsar of Russia.
1547-1584	Ivan the Terrible is tsar.
1613	The Romanov dynasty begins.
1689-1725	Peter the Great is tsar.
1695-1706	Russia fights the Ottoman Empire.
1700-1721	Russia fights Sweden.
1712	St. Petersburg becomes the new Russian capital.

EUROPE

Russians and Prussians

During the 18th century, eastern Europe was dominated by two very powerful rulers. Catherine the Great of Russia and Frederick the Great of Prussia both insisted that they should have complete power, and both of them used their power to make their countries rich and successful.

Catherine the Great

Catherine the Great was an intelligent and determined ruler who demanded total obedience from her people.

Catherine II became Tsarina (empress) of Russia in 1762, and ruled for more than 30 years. She encouraged Russian trade, set up universities, and invited thinkers and writers to her splendid court at St. Petersburg. Later, she became known as Catherine the Great.

New lands

Catherine's army won new land around the Black Sea and the Baltic Sea, and the Russians built ports on both of these coasts. But Russia's most important gains came from the break-up of the weak kingdom of Poland. Poland was split between Russia, Austria and Prussia, and Catherine made sure that Russia had the largest share.

Life in Russia

While Catherine and her courtiers lived in luxury, the Russian peasants paid heavy taxes and had to fight in the army. At first, Catherine planned to make life better for her people, but most of her plans were never put into action. Peasant rebellions were brutally crushed, and when Catherine drove through Russia, her officials paid wealthy farmers to pretend to be peasants so that she wouldn't see how poor her people really were.

In this scene, Tsarina Catherine is driving through the Russian countryside in her sleigh.

Catherine's sleigh passes well-built houses like this, but most Russian peasants live in tumbledown shacks.

Wealthy farmers in warm clothes wave at the tsarina.

An official pushes the real peasants out of sight.

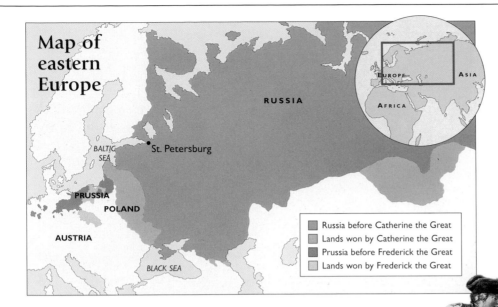

Map of eastern Europe

RUSSIA

St. Petersburg

BALTIC SEA

PRUSSIA

POLAND

AUSTRIA

BLACK SEA

EUROPE · ASIA · AFRICA

Russia before Catherine the Great
Lands won by Catherine the Great
Prussia before Frederick the Great
Lands won by Frederick the Great

Frederick's wars

Frederick the Great was a brilliant soldier who used his well-trained army to conquer large areas of land. He won outstanding victories against France and Austria in the Seven Years' War, and by the end of his reign he had doubled the size of Prussia.

This 18th-century painting shows a violent battle in the Seven Years' War.

The rise of Prussia

In 1618, the weak state of Prussia was inherited by the ruler of the German state of Brandenburg. Prussia's new rulers built up a strong army and united all their lands under an efficient government. In 1701, the ruler of Brandenburg was crowned King of Prussia, and an ambitious new country was born.

Frederick the Great

Frederick II, known as Frederick the Great, became King of Prussia in 1740. He was a talented musician, a brave general and a stern ruler who believed that only a king with total power could make a real difference to the lives of his people.

Frederick improved education for middle-class boys, encouraged the study of science, and helped to build up farming and trade in Prussia. He also made it illegal to torture prisoners, and allowed both Catholics and Protestants to follow their own religion.

Important dates

1701-1713	Frederick I is the first King of Prussia.
1740-1786	Frederick the Great is King of Prussia.
1756-1763	Prussia and Britain fight France, Russia and Austria in the Seven Years' War.
1762-1796	Catherine the Great is Tsarina of Russia.

EUROPE

Early Settlers in the Americas

Soon after Christopher Columbus reached America in 1492, the first settlers from Europe began arriving in the New World. By 1550, there were thousands of Spanish and Portuguese settlers in the West Indies and South America. At the same time, settlers from France had begun to make their homes in the land that is now called Canada.

Soldiers and priests

Spanish soldiers conquered large areas of South America and set up colonies with Spanish rulers, called viceroys. Some soldiers and priests from Spain also settled in North America, building forts and churches in Florida and California.

This 19th-century painting shows a lakeside town in the Spanish colony of New Granada.

Silver and gold

Spanish settlers opened up mines in Mexico and Peru, and sent back shiploads of silver and gold to Spain. The Spanish forced the Native Americans to work in their mines, and many workers died of exhaustion or disease.

Spanish cross made from South American gold

French settlers

The early French settlers in Canada built their homes close to rivers, and lived by trapping and hunting animals and catching fish. Slowly, the settlers spread out, and in 1699 they claimed all the land around the Mississippi River, naming the area Louisiana after the French king, Louis XIV.

Portuguese plantations

Portuguese settlers in Brazil grew sugar on vast farms called plantations, and brought slaves from Africa to work on their farms. (For more about slavery see pages 34 and 35.)

French losses

The French were not the only Europeans to settle in North America, and by 1700 the British also owned large areas of land. In 1754, the French and the British began fighting each other for land. At first, the French managed to fight off the British, but in 1759 British troops, led by General James Wolfe, captured the French city of Quebec. After this victory, the British won more land from France, and in 1763 the French signed the Peace of Paris, giving most of their land in Canada to Britain.

General James Wolfe

Map of the Americas

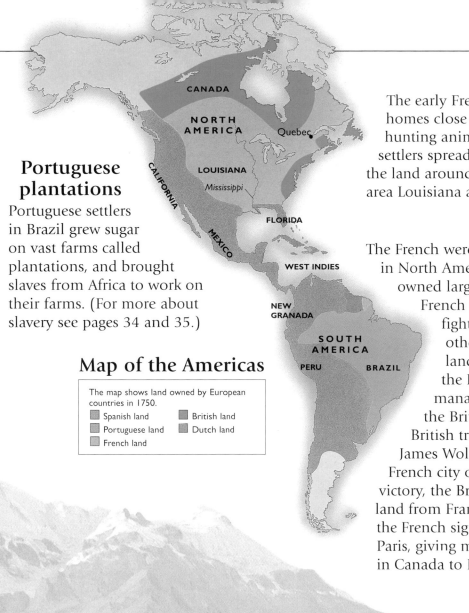

The map shows land owned by European countries in 1750.

- Spanish land
- Portuguese land
- French land
- British land
- Dutch land

Important dates

By 1600 The Spanish, Portuguese and French all have colonies in the Americas.

1699 The French create the colony of Louisiana.

1754 War breaks out in North America between the British and the French.

1759 The British capture Quebec.

1763 The Peace of Paris gives Britain control of Canada.

Settlers in North America

Near the end of the 16th century, groups of settlers from England tried to set up colonies on the east coast of North America. The first English settlers either died or returned home, but in 1607 a successful settlement was started in Jamestown, Virginia.

Pilgrim settlers

In August 1620, a group of English settlers set sail for Virginia in a ship called the *Mayflower*. The settlers belonged to a strict religious group who wanted to be free to worship God in their own way. Later, they became known as the Pilgrims, or the Pilgrim Fathers.

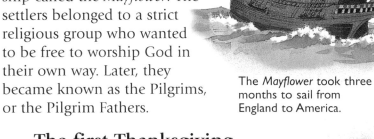

The *Mayflower* took three months to sail from England to America.

The first Thanksgiving

The *Mayflower* was blown off course and landed in a place that the Pilgrims named Plymouth. The first winter was extremely hard, but, with the help of the local Native Americans, half of the settlers survived.

After their first harvest, the Pilgrims made a simple meal and held a service of thanksgiving. Every November, many Americans remember this event with a Thanksgiving meal.

This picture shows the Pilgrims preparing their first Thanksgiving meal.

Land and freedom

By the 1650s, many settlers were sailing from Europe to North America. Groups of Puritans (strict Protestants) and Catholics settled in America so that they could be free to follow their own religion. But many other settlers left Europe in search of land and adventure.

New Amsterdam

In 1624, a group of Dutch settlers built a settlement on an island in the Hudson River and named it New Amsterdam. The Dutch controlled the island until 1664, when it was captured by the English, who renamed it New York.

These women are plucking wild turkeys.

Fish hung up to dry

House built from wooden planks, called clapboards

Some of the settlers are very weak and ill.

The Thirteen Colonies

By 1733, the British ruled 13 colonies on the east coast of America. The colonists grew tobacco, rice, and a blue dye called indigo. They sold these things to people in Europe in exchange for guns, clothes and tools.

Wars for land

At first, the settlers from Europe lived peacefully with the Native Americans, but as their colonies grew, battles for land began. By the 1720s, most of the native tribes on the east coast of America had been wiped out or had been driven west.

Map of the Thirteen Colonies

NORTH AMERICA

MASSACHUSETTS
NEW HAMPSHIRE
RHODE ISLAND
NEW YORK
Plymouth
CONNECTICUT
New York (New Amsterdam)
PENNSYLVANIA
NEW JERSEY
MARYLAND
DELAWARE
VIRGINIA
Jamestown
NORTH CAROLINA
SOUTH CAROLINA
GEORGIA

Native North Americans have taught the settlers how to fish, hunt and grow crops.

Fence to keep out wild animals

These Native Americans are bringing deer for the meal.

Chickens are kept for their eggs.

This woman is reading aloud from the Bible.

The settlers wear very plain clothes.

Important dates

1607	The English build a settlement in Jamestown, Virginia.
1620	The Pilgrims arrive in America.
1624	The Dutch settle in New Amsterdam.
By 1733	The British have 13 American colonies.

NORTH AMERICA

The Slave Trade

People had bought and sold slaves since ancient times, but in the 1580s this terrible trade increased dramatically. Millions of Africans were captured and sent across the ocean to the Americas. Those who survived the journey were sold as slaves, and most slaves had to work so hard they died within a few years.

Workers wanted

Since the 1500s, settlers from Europe had grown sugar and tobacco in the West Indies and South America. The settlers used native people to work on their vast farms, which were called plantations. However, by the 1550s, so many native people had died that the settlers were desperate for more workers.

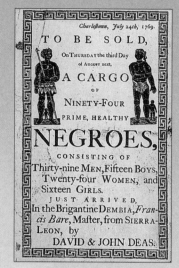

Charlestown, July 24th, 1769.
TO BE SOLD,
On Thursday the third Day
of August next,
A CARGO
OF
NINETY-FOUR
PRIME, HEALTHY
NEGROES,
CONSISTING OF
Thirty-nine MEN, Fifteen BOYS,
Twenty-four WOMEN, and
Sixteen GIRLS.
JUST ARRIVED,
In the Brigantine DEMBIA, *Francis Bare,* Master, from SIERRA-LEON, by
DAVID & JOHN DEAS.

The slave trade begins

The Portuguese had colonies on the west coast of Africa and they began to buy Africans who had been captured by rival tribes. The captives were chained together and forced to march to the coast. Then they were packed onto ships and sent to the Americas to be sold as slaves.

African slaves were sold to the buyer who offered the most money. Posters like this advertised the sales.

A triangle of trade

By 1600, many European countries had joined in the slave trade. Their ships made a three-stage journey in the shape of a triangle (see map opposite). First, the slave ships sailed from Europe to Africa, carrying goods such as guns and cloth. In Africa, they exchanged their goods for slaves, and sailed on to the Americas. There, the slaves were sold in exchange for sugar, tobacco and cotton before the ships returned to Europe. This triangle of trade made the slave traders extremely rich.

This 19th-century painting shows slaves from Africa working on a tobacco plantation in the West Indies.

Slave ships

Conditions on board the slave ships were appalling. The slaves were packed tightly together and were kept chained up in the dark for all of their eight-week voyage. Diseases spread rapidly on the ships, and more than a third of the slaves died before they even reached the Americas.

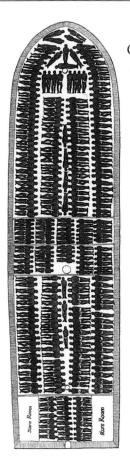

This diagram of a slave ship shows how tightly the slaves were packed together.

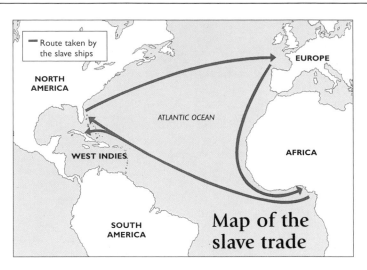

Map of the slave trade

Route taken by the slave ships

Slaves at work

Most slaves worked in the plantations of the West Indies and South America, but some of them were sent to the USA to pick cotton and harvest tobacco. A few masters were kind to their slaves, but many slaves were treated cruelly and forced to work very long hours.

Here is a family of slaves who worked in the cotton fields of the southern USA.

Slave rebellions

Some courageous slaves led rebellions against their masters, but most of these rebels were punished severely. In 1791, however, a successful revolt took place in Haiti in the West Indies, and the slaves' leader, Toussaint L'Ouverture, became ruler of Haiti.

Ending the slave trade

By the 1780s, many people in Europe had become unhappy about the slave trade. In 1792, Denmark became the first country to stop buying and selling slaves, and over the next 40 years the European slave trade slowly died out.

In 1804, slavery was banned in the northern states of the USA, but the people of the southern states continued to keep slaves for another 60 years. Gradually, slavery was made illegal all over the Americas, and the last slaves were set free in 1888.

Important dates

1680-1780	The slave trade is at its peak.
1792	Denmark stops its slave trade.
1804	Slavery is made illegal in the northern states of the USA.
1865	Slavery is made illegal throughout the USA.
1888	Slavery ends throughout the Americas.

THE WORLD

Exploring the South Seas

By the 1600s, European explorers had reached most parts of the world, but the South Pacific Ocean was still unknown. Sailors began to travel there, searching for new lands and riches.

Dutch explorers

In 1606, Dutch explorers reached the north coast of Australia, and in 1642 a Dutchman, Abel Tasman, sailed as far south as New Zealand. Tasman was also the first European to see the island of Tasmania, which was named after him.

Captain Cook

In 1768, Captain James Cook set out from Britain to explore the lands of the South Pacific. In some places, Cook's men were welcomed by the people who lived there. But when Cook's ship reached New Zealand, the native people, called Maoris, tried to frighten him away. Cook eventually made peace with the Maoris, and later drew detailed maps of New Zealand's coastline.

This picture shows Maori canoes approaching Captain Cook's ship, the *Endeavour*, as it arrives on the coast of New Zealand.

The ship is flying a British flag called the Red Ensign.

Scientists have come on the voyage to study wildlife in new lands.

Captain Cook

Cook's soldiers fire guns into the air, to drive the Maoris away.

The Maoris' canoes are covered with carvings.

AUSTRALASIA

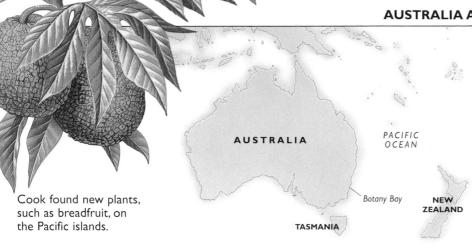

Cook found new plants, such as breadfruit, on the Pacific islands.

AUSTRALIA

PACIFIC OCEAN

Botany Bay

NEW ZEALAND

TASMANIA

Aboriginals

The people who lived in Australia before the Europeans arrived are known as Aboriginals. The Aboriginal people suffered terribly because of the new settlers. Many of them were killed by Europeans, and others died of diseases brought by the settlers.

A strange world

Cook arrived on the east coast of Australia in 1770, and claimed the country for Britain. He was amazed by the strange plants and animals he found, and named the place where he landed Botany Bay. (Botany is the study of plants.)

Map of the South Pacific

The British in New Zealand

Gradually, Europeans began to settle in New Zealand too. In 1840, the native Maoris agreed to let Britain have control over New Zealand. Later, Maori warriors tried to win back their lands. Many of them were killed in these battles, and their way of life began to disappear.

Maori warriors try to frighten Cook's men with a war dance.

Criminals and settlers

British people began arriving in Australia in the 1780s. Many were criminals who were sent there to work by the British government, but others were farmers looking for land. By the 1830s, about 100,000 Europeans were living in Australia.

Important dates

1606	Dutch explorers reach Australia.
1642	Abel Tasman reaches New Zealand.
1768-1779	Captain Cook leads three voyages to the South Seas.
1770	Captain Cook reaches Australia and claims it for Britain.
1788	Britain begins sending convicts to Australia.
1840	The British take control of New Zealand.

AUSTRALASIA

The British in India

During the 16th century, many merchants from Europe arrived in India. They bought silk, cotton, tea and spices, and built up wealthy trading companies.

Indian crocuses, and a spice called saffron which comes from their flowers

By the 1700s, India was split into areas ruled by local princes. The princes often fought each other, and the Europeans sometimes took sides in their battles.

Clive of India

In 1756, the Prince of Bengal captured a British trading base and killed more than a hundred people. The following year, a British general named Robert Clive led an army that defeated the Prince. Clive forced everyone in Bengal to pay taxes to the British East India Company, which became very powerful.

Robert Clive, who became rich by seizing gold that belonged to the Prince of Bengal

The rise of the British

The East India Company gradually built up a big army. It was led by British soldiers, but many Indians joined as well. The army defeated more and more princes, and took control of large areas of India.

This mechanical toy belonged to an Indian prince. It shows a tiger eating a British soldier.

The Indian Mutiny

Many Indian soldiers in the British army became angry. They felt that the British didn't respect Indian religions and were changing the country too much. In 1857, some Indian soldiers in Bengal began a mutiny, or rebellion, against the British.

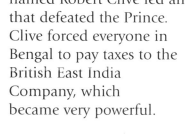

This scene is based on a 19th-century painting of a battle in the Indian Mutiny.

The fighting spread to many areas of northern India, but in 1858 the rebels were defeated. The British government took charge of the country, and India became an important part of the British Empire.

Princes and servants

After the mutiny, some Indian princes still lived in splendid palaces, but they no longer had any power. Most Indians remained poor, and many of them worked as servants for the British.

Making changes

The British built roads, railways and schools in India, and made the Indians learn English. Many British missionaries went to India and tried to persuade Indians to become Christians.

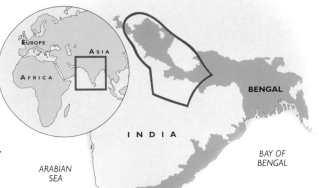

EUROPE

ASIA

AFRICA

BENGAL

INDIA

ARABIAN SEA

BAY OF BENGAL

Life in the Raj

By the 1880s, lots of British families were living in India. They tried to keep to a British way of life, but they were also influenced by Indian culture. The British stayed in India until 1947, when the country became independent. The period of time when the British ruled India is known as the Raj.

Map of India

- Areas controlled by the East India Company by 1805
— Main area where the Indian Mutiny took place

British people were not used to the hot Indian weather, and women used parasols to protect themselves from the sun.

This photograph shows King George V of Great Britain hunting tigers during a visit to India in 1911.

Important dates

1600   The British East India Company is created.

1757   Robert Clive defeats the Prince of Bengal at the Battle of Plassey.

1757-1857   Britain conquers large areas of India.

1857-1858   The Indian Mutiny

1858   The British government takes control of India.

SOUTH ASIA

39

The American Revolution

By the 1700s, Britain had 13 colonies on the east coast of North America (see page 33). The British government ruled its colonies with strict laws, and made the colonists pay more taxes than people in Britain. Many colonists thought that this was unfair, and riots broke out.

Map of the Thirteen Colonies

British colonies

NORTH AMERICA

Boston

ATLANTIC OCEAN

Yorktown

Tea in the sea

One very unpopular tax made it extremely expensive to buy tea in America. In 1773, colonists climbed on board ships delivering tea to the port of Boston and threw all the tea into the sea. This famous protest is known as the Boston Tea Party.

Fighting begins

The British government punished the colonists with even stricter laws, and moved a large army into North America. Fighting soon broke out between the colonists and the British.

Breaking free

The colonists began to think of themselves as Americans and wanted to break free from Britain. In 1776, the leaders of all 13 colonies signed a statement called the Declaration of Independence.

This painting shows the leaders of the colonies signing the Declaration of Independence.

The Declaration said that the colonies were now an independent country. The colonists called their new country the United States of America (USA).

Early battles

The British didn't want to lose control of their North American land, and they fought hard against the new American army. Although the Americans had a strong leader, named George Washington, the British soldiers were better trained and more experienced. The British won several early battles and captured some important cities.

George Washington, a skilled soldier and an inspiring leader

French friends

In 1777, France decided to support the USA against Britain. By this time, the American army was stronger and, with the help of the French, the Americans began to win more battles. In 1781, the British surrendered after a long battle at Yorktown, and the war was over.

Here you can see the American army attacking a British fort during the Battle of Yorktown. The Americans have started their attack at night, in order to take the British by surprise.

A new nation

Soon after the war, Britain signed a peace treaty and accepted the United States as an independent country. In 1787, a lawyer named Thomas Jefferson wrote a set of laws for the new country. These laws are known as the American Constitution. In 1789, George Washington was elected the first President of the USA.

The American flag has 13 stripes, one for each of the 13 colonies.

Americans from all 13 colonies fight alongside each other.

The American soldiers wear blue jackets.

American cannons have destroyed parts of the British wall.

The British have built a wall of soil and tree trunks to protect themselves.

This gun is called a musket.

Metal cannonballs

The British soldiers are known as "redcoats".

Important dates

1773	The Boston Tea Party
July 4, 1776	The 13 colonies declare independence.
1777	France joins the Americans in their war against Britain.
1781	Britain is defeated by the USA and France.
1787	The American Constitution is written.
1789	George Washington becomes the first President of the USA.

The French Revolution

By the 1780s, many French people were angry with their ruler, King Louis XVI, and the way he ran the country. Although the French government was running out of money, the king's nobles still led a luxurious life and paid no taxes. Meanwhile, the peasants and workers had to pay high taxes, and there wasn't enough work or food for them all.

Facing disaster

By 1789, the government had no money left at all, and France was in a desperate situation. In order to solve the country's problems, the king was forced to call a meeting of the Estates General, the French parliament, which had not met for almost 200 years.

Tax troubles

Some of those who came to the meeting of the Estates General were middle-class people, such as merchants and lawyers. Unlike the nobles, the middle classes had to pay taxes. They demanded that everyone should pay fair taxes, but the king refused. This made many French people furious.

Storming the Bastille

On July 14, 1789, a crowd of poor people, helped by some of the king's soldiers, attacked and captured an important prison in Paris, called the Bastille. This dramatic event is known as the storming of the Bastille.

In this scene, French rebels are attacking the Bastille. This was the start of the French Revolution.

A guard plummets from the battlements.

Cannonballs smash the prison walls.

The king's army has joined the rebels.

People shout and cheer.

The revolution spreads

The news that the Bastille had been captured encouraged many other people to rebel, and a revolution soon broke out all over France. The middle classes took control of the country, and in 1793 the king was executed.

Maximilien Robespierre, leader of the French people during the Reign of Terror

The Reign of Terror

The revolution quickly became very violent. The queen was executed, as well as thousands of nobles, and anyone else who was thought to be against the revolution. This frightening period became known as the Reign of Terror.

This is a guillotine, a machine used by the revolutionaries to execute their enemies.

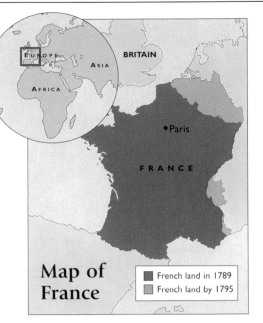

Map of France

■	French land in 1789
■	French land by 1795

War in Europe

The revolutionaries promised to help people in other nations to rebel against their rulers, and France began to invade nearby countries. Many European rulers were worried and wanted to stop the revolution. In 1793, several countries, such as Britain and Austria, attacked France, and war began. By 1795, the French had defeated most of their enemies and won new land in Europe.

Red, white and blue ribbons, like those worn by the French revolutionaries

Some buildings have been set on fire.

Rebels have broken through the prison gate.

Peasants use their farm tools as weapons.

Important dates

May 1789	Louis XVI calls a meeting of the Estates General.
July 14, 1789	The Bastille is captured by revolutionaries.
1793	Louis XVI is executed.
1793-1794	The Reign of Terror
1793-1795	France is at war with most of Europe.

EUROPE

43

The Empire of Napoleon

During the wars that followed the French Revolution, a brilliant young general named Napoleon Bonaparte won many battles for the French army. Napoleon became popular and powerful, and in 1799 he seized control of France.

New laws

Napoleon made many new laws, giving everyone in France the right to own land and to find a good job. However, he was also an extremely strict ruler who wanted as much power for himself as possible.

Napoleon the Emperor

In 1804, Napoleon made himself Emperor of France. His army won a series of spectacular victories, and by 1812 he had conquered most of western Europe. Napoleon ruled from Paris, and put his relatives in charge of parts of his empire.

Defeat at sea

One country that Napoleon failed to take over was Britain. Britain was hard to invade because it had a powerful navy. In 1805, British ships defeated the French navy just off Cape Trafalgar, in southern Spain. The British encouraged other countries to stand up to Napoleon.

Napoleon Bonaparte, painted in 1801 by the French artist Jacques Louis David

This 19th-century painting shows a scene from the Battle of Trafalgar.

The French and British ships have moved close together to fire at each other.

EUROPE

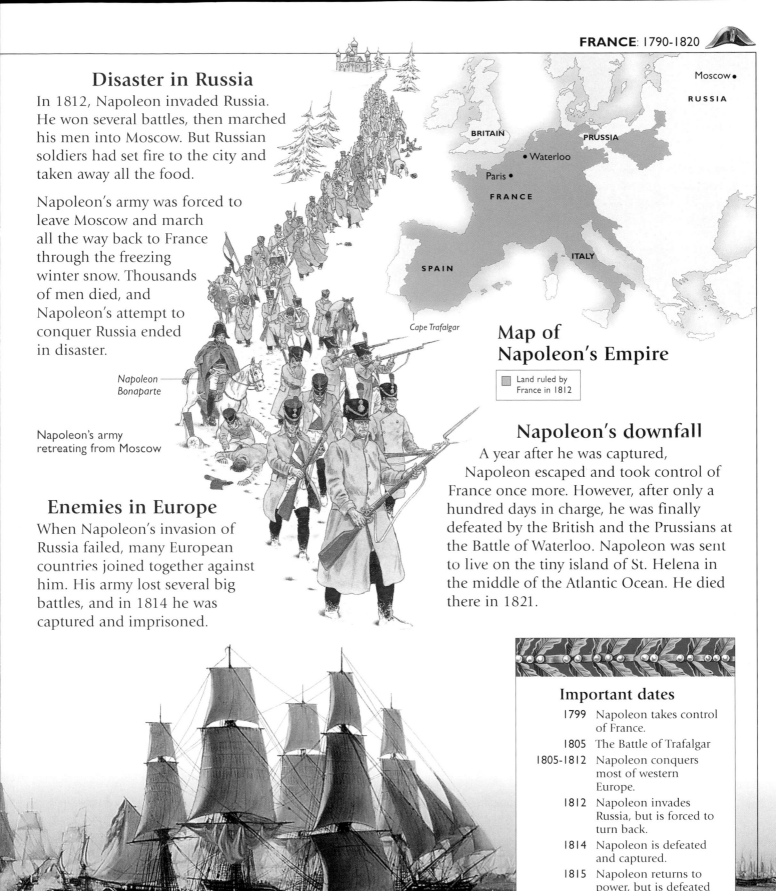

Disaster in Russia

In 1812, Napoleon invaded Russia. He won several battles, then marched his men into Moscow. But Russian soldiers had set fire to the city and taken away all the food.

Napoleon's army was forced to leave Moscow and march all the way back to France through the freezing winter snow. Thousands of men died, and Napoleon's attempt to conquer Russia ended in disaster.

Napoleon Bonaparte

Napoleon's army retreating from Moscow

Enemies in Europe

When Napoleon's invasion of Russia failed, many European countries joined together against him. His army lost several big battles, and in 1814 he was captured and imprisoned.

Moscow

RUSSIA

BRITAIN

PRUSSIA

• Waterloo

Paris •

FRANCE

ITALY

SPAIN

Cape Trafalgar

Map of Napoleon's Empire

◻ Land ruled by France in 1812

Napoleon's downfall

A year after he was captured, Napoleon escaped and took control of France once more. However, after only a hundred days in charge, he was finally defeated by the British and the Prussians at the Battle of Waterloo. Napoleon was sent to live on the tiny island of St. Helena in the middle of the Atlantic Ocean. He died there in 1821.

Important dates

1799	Napoleon takes control of France.
1805	The Battle of Trafalgar
1805-1812	Napoleon conquers most of western Europe.
1812	Napoleon invades Russia, but is forced to turn back.
1814	Napoleon is defeated and captured.
1815	Napoleon returns to power, but is defeated at Waterloo.
1815-1821	Napoleon is imprisoned on the island of St. Helena.

Changes in Farming

Until the late 1600s, farming in Europe had hardly changed for hundreds of years. Most families grew their own food on small strips of land in big fields that belonged to wealthy landowners. There were no farm machines, and people had to manage with just a few simple tools.

By 1700, new ideas and machines were being tried out on farms in Britain and the Netherlands. The new ideas soon spread across Europe, and the changes that they brought became known as the Agricultural Revolution.

Rotating crops

Planting the same crop in a field year after year wears out the soil, so farmers regularly left a field unplanted to let the soil recover. But in the 18th century, some farmers discovered that they could stop the soil from wearing out by planting a different crop in each field every year. This new system was called crop rotation. It meant that farmers could use all their fields all the time, and grow more food.

Corn

Turnip

Potatoes

New crops grown by European farmers in the 18th century

This scene shows how a British farming village might have looked by the year 1800.

Wheat has been planted in this field. Next year, turnips will be grown here.

Manure (animal dung) is spread on the land to help crops grow.

Village inn

Village shop

This man is making deep furrows (grooves) in the field.

A seed drill is used to plant seeds in the furrows.

This open space is called the village green.

The landowner rides around the village, inspecting his land.

Planting seeds

One of the most important new machines was the seed drill, which was invented by an English farmer named Jethro Tull. Instead of scattering seeds onto the ground by hand, people could use the seed drill to drop seeds straight into the soil. This meant that far fewer seeds were blown away or eaten by birds.

EUROPE

46

Better breeding

Some farmers began using only their biggest, healthiest animals for breeding. These animals often had big babies, and over time farm animals became larger, so they could feed more people.

Wealthy farmers had pictures painted that made their animals, such as this sheep, look even bigger than they were.

Fields and fences

Some British landowners realized that it was more practical to grow crops in large fields than in lots of small strips. They took over the strips of land where families had grown their own food and put them together to make bigger fields for themselves.

The landowners built fences and planted hedges around their fields, and villagers were forbidden to use these fields. This meant that many people no longer had anywhere to grow their food, so they had to work for a landowner or find a job in a town.

The vicar, or priest, lives in this house.

Church

This house belongs to the wealthy landowner who owns most of the land in the village.

The land has been divided into fields for the landowner.

Hedges have been planted around the fields.

Blacksmith's workshop

The landowner built these cottages for villagers who work for him.

Steam power

By the 1850s, some farmers were using new steam-powered machines (see page 48). The machines helped to harvest crops, dig the fields and pump water out of marshy land.

Here are some farm workers with a steam-powered machine for threshing crops. The machine separates the grain from the stalks.

This family is leaving to find work in a town.

The Industrial Revolution

I n the 18th century, many changes began to take place in the way that people lived and worked in Britain. These changes later spread across the world, and together they became known as the Industrial Revolution.

Mining coal

Steam for the new engines came from boiling water, and huge amounts of coal were needed to heat the water. Deep coal mines were dug, and men, women and children worked in the mines. Working underground was very dangerous, and many people were killed or injured.

Children working in a coal mine

New machines

In 1700, most people in Britain lived in villages. Many villagers worked on farms, but others worked at home, spinning wool and cotton thread, then weaving the thread into cloth.

This way of life began to change in the 1700s, when British inventors first designed machines that could spin and weave cloth very quickly. The machines were too big and expensive for people to use at home, so wealthy businessmen built factories that could hold lots of machines.

This machine, called a Spinning Jenny, could spin 16 threads at once, instead of just one.

Steam power

At first, running water was used to turn the wheels that made the machines work, so all the factories had to be built near rivers. Then, in 1782, James Watt invented a powerful engine that was driven by steam. Hundreds of these new steam-engines were built to run machines in factories all over Britain.

Factories and towns

Busy towns soon grew up around the factories, as thousands of people moved out of their villages to work on the new machines. People had to work very long hours, and many workers were injured while using the machines.

During the Industrial Revolution, iron was used to make engines, boats, trains and bridges. This is the world's first iron bridge, built at Coalbrookdale in England in 1779.

Canals and trains

Roads were muddy and bumpy in the 18th century, and carts were often attacked by robbers, so factory owners had to find a different way to transport their goods. For many years, they used canals, but canal boats were slow. Then, early in the 19th century, British inventors discovered how to build steam-powered trains. This made it much easier to travel long distances.

The *Rocket*, a famous early steam train, designed by George Stephenson

The Rocket could travel at up to 50km (30 miles) an hour.

Britain booms

Here you can see inside the Crystal Palace, which was built to contain the Great Exhibition of 1851.

Britain had so many factories that it became known as "the workshop of the world", and by the 1800s it was an extremely rich and powerful country. In 1851, many British inventors displayed their machines at a huge event in London, known as the Great Exhibition. Millions of people came from around the world to admire the new inventions.

The machine-smashers

The new machines worked so fast that people who made cloth at home couldn't earn a living. This made some people angry, and they tried to destroy the machines. The most famous machine-smashers were the Luddites, named after their leader Ned Ludd.

However, protesters like the Luddites could do nothing to stop the Industrial Revolution, and the number of factories continued to grow.

A Luddite

Important dates

1767	James Hargreaves invents the Spinning Jenny.
1782	James Watt invents a powerful steam engine.
1804	Richard Trevithick builds the first steam train to run along a track.
1811	The Luddites start smashing machines.
1825	Passenger trains start running in Britain.
1829	George Stephenson builds the *Rocket*.
1851	The Great Exhibition

EUROPE

49

Life in the New Towns

By the 1850s, there were factories in many parts of Britain, and large, busy towns were growing up around them. Although the factory owners became rich and lived in grand houses, the workers were paid very little and were extremely poor. They lived in dirty, crowded parts of the town, known as slums.

This scene shows part of a British town around 1850.

Life in the slums

Factory workers lived in rows of tiny houses on narrow streets. Their houses had no inside toilets or running water, the air was full of smoke from the factories, and the streets were filthy, so diseases spread quickly. There was a lot of crime, because some poor people had to steal food or money to survive.

Thick smoke from the factories pollutes the air.

Cloth factory

Up to 20 people live in each tiny house.

Gas lamp

The factory owner drives past quickly.

Ditch full of smelly waste

This policeman is chasing a thief.

People get water from a pump in the street, called a standpipe.

This boy is a chimney sweep. He earns money by climbing inside chimneys to clean them.

Wealthy people, such as lawyers and businessmen, live in larger houses on the edge of town.

Steam train

Houses are built back-to-back and in rows.

Outhouse for toilet

Workhouses

People who had no money or who couldn't work were sent to live in places called workhouses, which were almost like prisons. Once inside the workhouse, people had to work very long hours, and it was hard to get out again. Families were split up and hardly ever allowed to see each other.

The workers protest

Many workers, like these matchmakers, became ill because of the dangerous chemicals they had to handle.

Lots of factory workers felt they were being treated unfairly, so they started to form groups, called trade unions. The unions demanded better pay, shorter hours and safer places to work.

At first, trade unions were banned by the government, but in 1825 they became legal. When the members of a union wanted to protest about something, they all agreed to stop working and go on strike.

Making changes

Members of the trade unions and some wealthy people put pressure on the government to make life better for the poor. In the second half of the 19th century, factories became safer, and better houses were built. New drains and sewers made the streets cleaner, which helped to prevent diseases from spreading.

Going to school

In 1800, parents usually had to pay to send their children to school, so many children from poor families never learned to read or write. Over the next hundred years, laws were passed which allowed children to have a free education. By 1900, all children had to go to school until the age of 12. Schools were very strict, and pupils were often beaten by their teachers.

A group of children from the slums of London

The Year of Revolutions

By 1848, various groups of people in Europe had become unhappy with their rulers, and wanted more say in how their countries were run. In many places, there weren't enough jobs for everyone, and people were desperately short of food. They remembered the French Revolution of 1789, and thought they could solve their problems with more revolutions.

A year of chaos

In February 1848, a rebellion broke out in Paris and the rebels took control of France. When people in other countries heard about this, a wave of revolutions swept across Europe, and 1848 became known as the Year of Revolutions.

By the end of 1849, the revolutions had been crushed and most of the old rulers were back in power. However, rulers all over Europe realized that they would have to pay more attention to their people in the future.

New ideas

At the same time as the revolutions were spreading through Europe, some powerful new ideas were beginning to change the way people thought.

In 1848, a British group called the Chartists demanded that men of all classes should have the right to vote. In the same year, a German thinker named Karl Marx wrote a book called *The Communist Manifesto*. This said that workers everywhere should unite to gain more power for themselves.

Karl Marx and the title page of *The Communist Manifesto*

The rebels used whatever they could find to build barriers, or barricades, in the streets. This is part of a poster showing French rebels defending a barricade.

New Nations

At the start of the 19th century, the countries now known as Greece, Italy and Germany did not exist. Germany and Italy were made up of lots of small states, and some of these states were ruled by foreign countries. Greece was part of the Turkish Ottoman Empire.

The nation of Greece

In 1827, the Greeks who lived in the Ottoman Empire decided to join together to fight against their Turkish rulers. The rebels defeated the Turks and formed the independent kingdom of Greece.

Greek soldiers fighting for independence

Italy unites

By 1859, the Italian states of Piedmont and Sardinia, led by Count Camillo Cavour, had taken control of most of northern Italy. At the same time, a soldier named Giuseppe Garibaldi led an army of rebels that conquered large areas of southern Italy. In 1860, Count Cavour and Garibaldi agreed to join the north and south of the country together, and a year later the new nation of Italy was created.

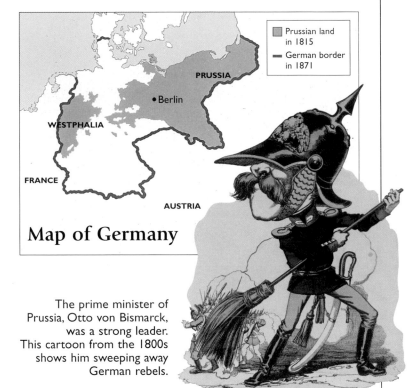

Map of Germany

- Prussian land in 1815
- German border in 1871

The prime minister of Prussia, Otto von Bismarck, was a strong leader. This cartoon from the 1800s shows him sweeping away German rebels.

Germany unites

By 1815, the most powerful German state was Prussia, governed by King Wilhelm I and his prime minister, Otto von Bismarck. Prussia already ruled Westphalia, and gradually took control of many other German states. Prussia also won impressive victories against Austria and France, and in 1871 the rest of the states decided to join the growing nation. Germany was united and Wilhelm became its first emperor, or kaiser.

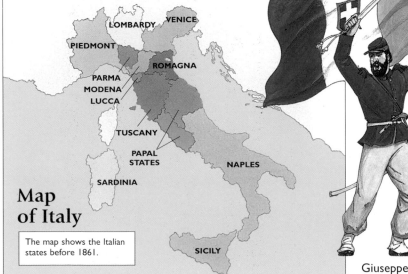

Map of Italy

The map shows the Italian states before 1861.

Giuseppe Garibaldi

Important dates

1827   Greece becomes an independent country.

1848   Revolutions in many parts of Europe

1861   The Italian states join together to form Italy.

1871   Germany is united under Wilhelm I.

EUROPE

Revolutions in South America

Since the 16th century, Spain and Portugal had owned vast colonies in South America. The colonies were ruled by a few rich landowners, but most South Americans were poor.

Fighting for freedom

By the 1800s, many South Americans wanted to break free from their foreign rulers and form their own nations. Portugal allowed Brazil to become a separate country in 1822, but the Spanish were determined to keep control of their land. This meant that all the Spanish colonies had to fight for their independence.

Bolivar the rebel

The most famous South American rebel leader was Simon Bolivar, from the northern colony of Venezuela. Bolivar became commander of Venezuela's rebel army in 1811, and fought the Spanish for three years, before being defeated.

This is a portrait of Simon Bolivar. He was determined to free South America from Spanish rule.

Across the mountains

Bolivar realized he couldn't beat the huge Spanish army in Venezuela, so he planned a surprise attack on the nearby colony of New Granada. In 1819, he led his soldiers on a dangerous journey over the Andes mountains and into New Granada. There, he defeated the Spanish army and helped the colony to become an independent nation, known today as Colombia.

People in New Granada celebrating independence with Bolivar's soldiers

Flag of New Granada

These peaks in Venezuela are part of the Andes mountains. Simon Bolivar and his army crossed these huge mountains on their way to New Granada.

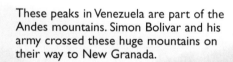

Defeating the Spanish

Bolivar spent the next few years moving around South America, fighting the Spanish in different colonies. In 1821, he finally freed his home colony of Venezuela, and the next year he drove the Spanish out of Ecuador.

San Martín strikes

Another great rebel leader was José de San Martín, who led Chile and Argentina to independence. He also freed most of Peru, where the Spanish had been especially powerful.

A 19th-century painting
of José de San Martín

Peru and Bolivia

In 1824, Simon Bolivar drove the Spanish from the rest of Peru. He then made part of Peru into a new nation, which was named Bolivia after him.

Freedom and war

By 1830, all of the South American colonies had become independent. However, in the years that followed, many wars broke out between the new nations, and life remained hard for the people of South America.

Map of South America

☐ Spanish land in 1800

■ Portuguese land in 1800

Map labels: ATLANTIC OCEAN, VENEZUELA, GUIANA, NEW GRANADA (COLOMBIA), ECUADOR, BRAZIL, PERU, BOLIVIA, PARAGUAY, CHILE, URUGUAY, ARGENTINA

Important dates

1808	Some South American colonies start fighting against the Spanish.
1816-1824	Bolivar and San Martín help to win independence for many colonies.
1822	Portugal declares Brazil an independent country.
1825	Bolivar creates the country of Bolivia.
By 1830	All the South American colonies are independent.

SOUTH AMERICA

The Scramble for Africa

For hundreds of years, the vast continent of Africa was divided into kingdoms led by powerful African rulers. In 1652, the Dutch conquered an area called Cape Colony in the south, and by the 1800s French, British and Portuguese traders had settled along the coast. However, most of Africa was still unknown to Europeans.

Things began to change in the 19th century, when European countries tried to win land for their empires. The Europeans also hoped to find gold and precious stones in Africa, and they competed fiercely against each other. This struggle became known as the Scramble for Africa.

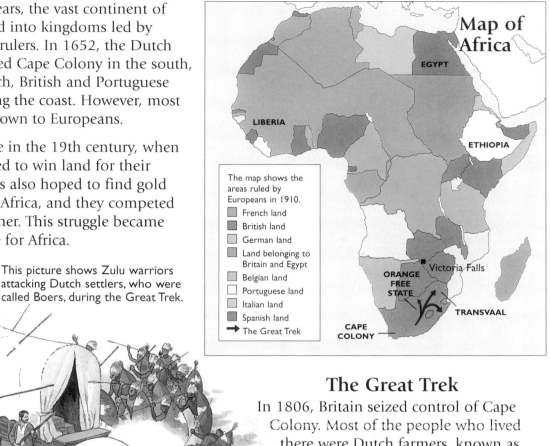

Map of Africa

The map shows the areas ruled by Europeans in 1910.

- French land
- British land
- German land
- Land belonging to Britain and Egypt
- Belgian land
- Portuguese land
- Italian land
- Spanish land
- → The Great Trek

EGYPT

LIBERIA

ETHIOPIA

Victoria Falls

ORANGE FREE STATE

TRANSVAAL

CAPE COLONY

This picture shows Zulu warriors attacking Dutch settlers, who were called Boers, during the Great Trek.

The Boers shelter behind their wagons.

The Zulus fight with spears.

Thorn bushes protect the wagons.

The Great Trek

In 1806, Britain seized control of Cape Colony. Most of the people who lived there were Dutch farmers, known as Boers, and they soon became very unhappy with their new British rulers.

In 1836, thousands of Boers set off on a long journey in search of a different place to live. This journey became known as the Great Trek. Eventually, the Boers took over some land and set up two colonies, called the Transvaal and the Orange Free State.

The Zulu wars

The African people whose land the Boers seized were called the Zulus. For many years, Zulu warriors tried to win back their homeland by fighting bravely against the Boers. But the British helped the Boers, and the Zulus were defeated in 1879.

Exploring Africa

Although Europeans had settled on the African coast, many of them were scared of the deadly diseases and wild animals that they thought they would find inland. However, a few brave explorers went on dangerous expeditions. The most famous was the Christian missionary David Livingstone, who explored large parts of Africa and made maps of the land.

Europe moves in

By the 1880s, many European countries had begun to win land in Africa. The new nations of Italy and Germany were especially eager to build up empires for themselves, and soon the Europeans had conquered huge areas of the continent. Any Africans who tried to fight back were killed.

Europe takes over

In 1884, European leaders met in Berlin and decided to divide up Africa between them. Each country took over a different part of the continent, until eventually only Ethiopia and Liberia were still ruled by Africans (see map). Many Africans were treated very badly by their new rulers, and they often rebelled against the Europeans.

The Boer War

Here are some Boer soldiers. Most of the soldiers were not very well trained, but they fought hard to defend their land.

Despite the Europeans' agreement in Berlin, they continued fighting over land. In 1899, Britain tried to take over the Dutch colonies, and war broke out between the British and the Boers. The British imprisoned many Boers and destroyed their farms, and the Boers were forced to surrender. In 1902, the Boers' land became part of the British Empire.

This is Victoria Falls, in southern Africa. The British explorer David Livingstone was the first European to see the Falls, in 1855.

Important dates

1806	Britain takes control of Cape Colony.
1836-1845	The Great Trek
1841	David Livingstone starts to explore Africa.
1879	The Zulus are defeated.
1884	European leaders divide Africa between them.
1902	The British defeat the Boers. Transvaal and the Orange Free State become part of the British Empire.

The American Civil War

In the middle of the 19th century, the north and south of the United States seemed like two different countries. In the north, there were lots of big cities and factories, while most of the south was farmland.

Slavery in the south

In the southern states, the two most important crops were cotton and tobacco, which were grown on vast farms, called plantations. Thousands of people had been brought from Africa to work as slaves on these plantations. But slavery was banned in the north, and this led to bitter arguments with the people of the south.

The USA splits

In 1860, Abraham Lincoln was elected President of the United States. Lincoln was against slavery, and this made many people in the south angry. A group of southern states decided to break away and form their own independent country.

Map of the USA in 1861

Gettysburg
Bull Run
Atlanta
ATLANTIC OCEAN

■ Union states
■ Confederate states
■ Important civil war battles

The war begins

The American government told the southern states that they had no right to become a separate country, and in 1861 civil war broke out. For four years, the south, known as the Confederacy, struggled against the north, called the Union.

The Union had more soldiers and better weapons, but the Confederacy had brilliant generals, and the southern troops fought fiercely for their independence. The south won many battles in the early part of the war.

Robert E. Lee, an outstanding Confederate general

This is Abraham Lincoln. He was a strong leader who was determined to keep the United States together.

The Union advances

In 1863, Union troops won an important battle at Gettysburg, in the state of Pennsylvania. After this victory, Union armies began to advance into the south, burning and destroying all the farms and towns they found. Union ships surrounded the southern ports and prevented the Confederacy from bringing in more food and weapons.

This scene shows Union soldiers destroying a southern town.

The end of the war

Soon, the Confederate troops became weak and hungry. By 1865, large areas of the south had been destroyed, and the Confederacy surrendered. The war was over, but it had cost the lives of hundreds of thousands of soldiers on both sides.

Confederate flag

A difficult peace

After the civil war, the United States became a single nation once again. Slavery was made illegal, and thousands of black slaves were freed. However, there were still problems between the north and south. Five days after the war ended, Abraham Lincoln was assassinated by an angry Confederate supporter, and black people continued to be treated appallingly in many parts of the south.

Important buildings, such as factories and banks, have been set on fire.

This soldier is waving the Union flag.

Union soldiers smash the railway line to stop the Confederacy from transporting supplies.

Important dates

1860	Abraham Lincoln becomes President of the United States.
April 1861	Civil war breaks out.
1863	The Battle of Gettysburg
1863-1865	Union armies destroy many southern towns.
April 1865	The civil war ends. Lincoln is murdered.

NORTH AMERICA

The Growth of the USA

By the start of the 1800s, the United States of America was a large and growing nation. Over the next hundred years, the USA won huge areas of land, and millions of people came to settle in this exciting new country.

Buying land

Since 1700, France had owned the enormous colony of Louisiana in the middle of the North American continent, but in 1803 the US government bought it from the French. This dramatic deal is known as the Louisiana Purchase, and it doubled the size of the USA. Americans began to settle on this new land and set up new states there.

War with Mexico

Many people from the USA settled in a southern area called Texas, which was owned by the country of Mexico. In 1835, the Texans declared that they were independent from Mexico. The Mexicans fought to keep Texas, but after two years they were defeated. In 1845, Texas joined the USA.

This is Davy Crockett, who fought for Texas against the Mexicans. He was killed in the Battle of the Alamo at the town of San Antonio, in Texas.

Moving west

Gradually, people moved farther and farther west, and the government encouraged settlers, known as pioneers, to make their homes there. When gold was discovered in California in 1848, many people rushed to live in the area, hoping to make a fortune.

Pioneers heading for California during the Gold Rush

Lots of families travel together in groups of wagons, called wagon trains.

This photograph shows a rocky valley in the state of Utah, one of the places the pioneers passed through on their difficult journey to the West.

REWARD
(\$5,000.00)
Reward for the capture, dead or alive,
of one Wm. Wright, better known as
"BILLY THE KID"
Age, 18. Height, 5 feet, 3 inches.
Weight, 125 lbs. Light hair, blue
eyes and even features. He is
the leader of the worst band of
desperadoes the Territory has
ever had to deal with. The above
reward will be paid for his capture
or positive proof of his death.
JIM DALTON, Sheriff.
**DEAD OR ALIVE!
BILLY THE KID**

The Wild West

For many years, the American West was a wild and dangerous place, full of crooks and bandits.

This poster from the 1870s offers a huge reward to anyone who captures the famous bandit Billy the Kid.

Map of the USA

- ■ United States in 1800
- □ Land gained in the Louisiana Purchase
- ■ Land gained by 1900
- — One route taken by pioneers

Cattle herders, or cowboys, drove cattle over the plains to be loaded onto trains and sold in the east. There were many clashes between the cowboys and the Native Americans who lived on the plains.

Taking land

As the USA grew bigger, settlers moved into many areas where Native Americans lived. At first, the government promised to leave the Native Americans alone, but most of their land was gradually taken away.

Struggling to survive

Some tribes of Native Americans refused to leave their land, and they fought hard against the settlers and the US army. The Native Americans won some battles, but many tribes were completely wiped out. US troops and settlers also killed most of the buffalo that roamed the plains, leaving the remaining tribes with very little to eat. By 1890, many Native Americans had been captured and were forced to live in camps guarded by US soldiers.

A new world power

By the 1890s, the USA stretched all the way from the Atlantic Ocean to the Pacific. Despite the wars against the Native Americans, and the terrible civil war in the 1860s, the country became extremely successful.

The USA was soon growing more crops and building more machines than any other country. By the beginning of the 20th century, it was one of the biggest, richest and most powerful nations in the world.

Sitting Bull, a Native American chief who fought the US army

Important dates

1803	The Louisiana Purchase
1835-1836	War between Texas and Mexico
1836	Battle of the Alamo
1848	Gold is found in California.
1860-1890	Native Americans fight the US army for land.
1876	Native Americans win the Battle of Little Bighorn.
1890	The Native Americans are finally defeated at the Battle of Wounded Knee.

NORTH AMERICA

The Ming and the Ch'ing

The vast empire of China was ruled by powerful emperors for thousands of years. In the 14th century, a new family, or dynasty, took control of China. They were called the Ming dynasty, and their emperors ruled for the next 280 years.

The Forbidden City

The Ming emperors governed from the northern city of Beijing, where they lived in a fabulous walled palace, called the Forbidden City. Only the emperor's family and advisers were allowed to enter the palace.

Art and medicine

During the Ming period, the Chinese made exquisite vases and elegant wooden furniture. They also designed amazing gardens and made beautifully illustrated books. Doctors treated their patients by sticking lots of needles into their skin. This treatment is called acupuncture and it is still used today.

This photograph shows the Hall of Supreme Harmony in the middle of the Forbidden City.

China and the world

By 1500, China was almost completely cut off from the rest of the world. The Ming emperors thought all foreigners were savages, and wanted to keep them out of China. Foreign merchants were only allowed to trade at a few Chinese ports.

Problems for the Ming

For a long time, China was peaceful, but problems began in the 16th century. The south coast was plagued by Japanese pirates and smugglers, and tribes from Mongolia often attacked northern China. To defend themselves against these attacks, the Ming emperors strengthened the Great Wall of China, which had been built in ancient times, and used thousands of soldiers to guard it.

A decorated jar from the Ming period

Chinese rebels

By the 1630s, many Chinese people were angry with the government, because there wasn't enough food for everyone and people were forced to pay heavy taxes. Rebellions broke out in many areas, and the country was thrown into chaos.

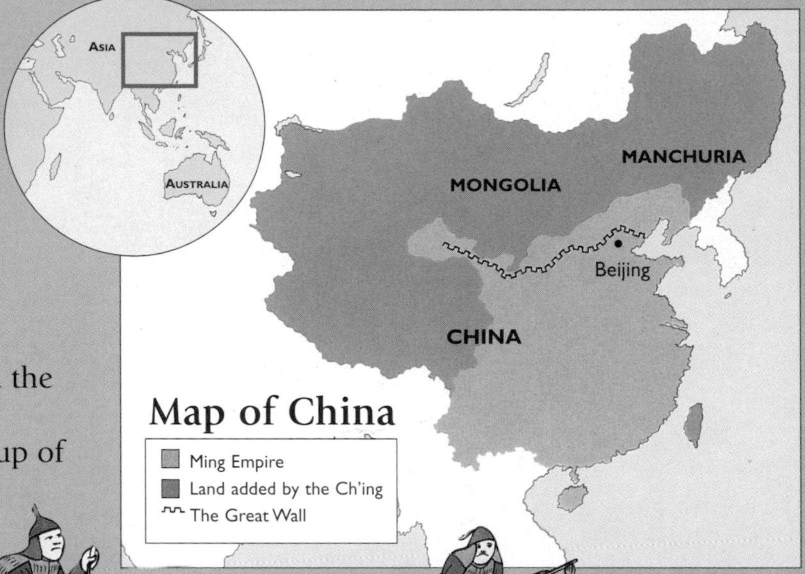

Attack of the Manchus

In 1644, rebels seized the city of Beijing, and the last Ming emperor committed suicide. The emperor's advisers asked the Manchus, a group of people from the north, to help them crush the rebellion. But the Manchus took advantage of the Ming's problems and took over Beijing. The Manchus gradually won more land, and by 1681 they had conquered all of China.

Map of China

ASIA

AUSTRALIA

MONGOLIA

MANCHURIA

Beijing

CHINA

Ming Empire

Land added by the Ch'ing

The Great Wall

Manchu warriors, painted by a Chinese artist

The Ch'ing dynasty

The Manchus started a new line of rulers, known as the Ch'ing dynasty, which lasted until 1912. The Manchu emperors won vast areas of new land to the north and west. They also made sure that China stayed independent from the rest of the world.

Changes in China

In the 18th century, European merchants were eager to buy Chinese goods, such as silk and tea. But China's Manchu emperors wanted to keep foreigners out of their country, so Europeans were only allowed to trade at the port of Canton.

K'ang Hsi, a powerful Manchu emperor

Silver and opium

The Manchu emperors made European traders pay Chinese merchants with silver, which was very costly for the Europeans. But in the 1720s, the British began paying the Chinese with a drug called opium instead.

Many Chinese people smoked opium, but the emperors disapproved of this, and in 1813 smoking opium was banned. However, the British continued selling opium to Chinese merchants, and this made the Manchu government angry.

The Opium War

In 1839, a government official burned thousands of chests of opium, and the emperor banned all trade with Britain. This made the British furious, and they attacked China. The British had much better ships and weapons, and they easily defeated the Chinese navy. After losing the war, China was forced to allow British merchants to trade at lots of Chinese ports.

This 19th-century British painting shows Chinese ships being destroyed by the British during the Opium War.

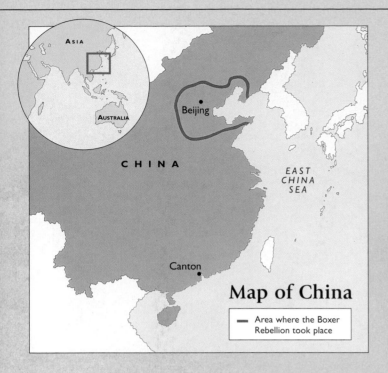

ASIA

Beijing

AUSTRALIA

CHINA

EAST
CHINA
SEA

Canton

Map of China

— Area where the Boxer
Rebellion took place

The Taiping Rebellion

The Manchu emperors also faced other problems during the 19th century. Their government had become weak, and in the 1850s a violent revolution, known as the Taiping Rebellion, broke out. For more than ten years, peasants all over China attacked their rulers and destroyed cities. By the time the Manchu emperor regained control in 1864, up to 20 million people had been killed.

Trying to change

Some Chinese people thought China could only overcome its problems by becoming more like a modern European country. They encouraged the government to build lots of factories and trains, but change was slow.

The Boxer Rebellion

Many people in China hated the way that Europeans had changed their country. In 1900, a secret society of warriors, known as the Boxers, started attacking Europeans and Chinese Christians.

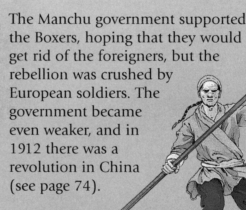

The Manchu government supported the Boxers, hoping that they would get rid of the foreigners, but the rebellion was crushed by European soldiers. The government became even weaker, and in 1912 there was a revolution in China (see page 74).

Boxer warriors like these thought they were protected by magic powers.

The Europeans advance

Soon, other European countries began forcing the Chinese to trade with them. They moved soldiers into China and took control of many ports. The Europeans wanted to persuade the Chinese to become Christians, so they began to send missionaries to China.

Important dates

1368-1644	The Ming dynasty
1644-1912	The Manchu dynasty
1839-1842	The Opium War
1850-1864	The Taiping Rebellion
1900	The Boxer Rebellion

THE FAR EAST

Changes in Japan

Map of Japan

At the start of the 16th century, Japan was in the middle of a long civil war. Fierce warlords, called samurai, fought each other for land, and the Japanese emperor had very little power.

Strong samurai

The civil war ended in 1568 when the powerful samurai Oda Nobunaga took control of Japan. After him, another samurai, Toyotomi Hideyoshi, became chief minister of Japan. Hideyoshi set up an efficient tax system and worked hard to create a united country.

The first Tokugawa

After Hideyoshi's death, war broke out again. Ieyasu Tokugawa defeated his rivals at the Battle of Sekigahara, and in 1603 the emperor made him shogun (military commander) of Japan.

This is Osaka Castle, which was seized by Ieyasu Tokugawa from a rival samurai.

The Edo period

While the emperor stayed in his palace in Kyoto, Tokugawa set up his capital in Edo. This was the start of a long line of Tokugawa shoguns who ruled Japan on behalf of the emperor. The Tokugawas controlled Japan for over 250 years, and this period of time became known as the Edo period.

Japan's isolation

In the 1630s, the shogun Iemitsu Tokugawa became frightened that European merchants and priests in Japan had too much influence over his people. He banned Christianity and declared that only the Dutch and Chinese were allowed to trade with Japan. Foreigners could not set foot on Japanese soil, so the Dutch had to trade from an island in Nagasaki Bay.

Peace and wealth

Japan remained cut off from the world for over 200 years. During this time, the Tokugawas ruled very strictly and made sure that there were no more civil wars in their country. Japanese towns grew fast, and Edo became one of the largest cities in the world. As the towns grew, Japanese traders became wealthy, but the peasants and samurai didn't share in this wealth. By the 1800s, there were many rebellions against the Tokugawa family.

Contact with the west

In 1854, a group of American warships waited in Edo Bay while their commander, Commodore Perry, forced the shogun to sign a trading agreement with the USA. Other agreements followed, and by 1860 Japan had started to trade with several western countries.

The end of the Tokugawas

Most of the samurai hated the western traders and blamed the Tokugawas for allowing them in. Civil war broke out, and in 1867 a samurai army defeated the Tokugawas. In 1868, the victorious samurai helped the Japanese emperor to take control of Japan. This is known as the Meiji Restoration. The emperor moved from Kyoto to Edo, which he renamed Tokyo.

Even in the 1800s, the samurai still wore their traditional costumes. In this 19th-century Japanese print, two samurai warriors are fighting each other.

Modernization

The Japanese began building steam trains in the 1880s. Here are two engine drivers in front of their train.

In spite of the samurai's hopes, the emperors continued trading with the West and copied many western ideas. They set up a parliament, improved schools, and built factories, trains and ships. Meanwhile, the samurai lost most of their power, and most of them had to do ordinary jobs.

Japanese wars

In 1894, Japan tried to conquer Korea, and this led to war with China. The Japanese won an easy victory, but in 1904 they had to fight the Russians for control of Korea. Once again, the Japanese were victorious. In 1905, the Treaty of Portsmouth gave Japan control of Korea and some land in China. This made Japan the most powerful country in the Far East.

Important dates

1568-1582	Oda Nobunaga controls Japan.
1591-1598	Toyotomi Hideyoshi controls Japan.
1603-1867	The Tokugawa shoguns rule Japan (the Edo period).
1854	Japan signs a trading agreement with the USA.
1868	The emperor takes control of Japan (the Meiji Restoration).
1894-1895	Japan fights China.
1904-1905	Japan fights Russia.
1905	The Treaty of Portsmouth gives Japan control of Korea.

The First World War

World War I, also known as the Great War, involved more countries and killed more people than any other war that had ever been fought before. But how did it all start?

Friends and enemies

By 1914, the five strongest countries in Europe had split into two rival groups. Britain, France and Russia (called the Allies) were on one side, with Germany and Austria-Hungary (called the Central Powers) on the other. The situation became very tense. If a war were to start between any two rival countries, all the others would probably join in.

Murder in Sarajevo

The event that actually sparked off the war took place on June 28, 1914. Archduke Franz Ferdinand, the heir to the Austrian throne, was visiting the town of Sarajevo in Bosnia, when he was shot dead by a Serbian student.

On July 28, Austria, backed up by Germany, declared war on Serbia. Russia stepped in to help the Serbs, and soon the Allies and the Central Powers were at war.

The Western Front

German soldiers moved quickly into northern France, but they were soon stopped by the Allies. The two sides faced each other along a line known as the Western Front. Both sides dug deep ditches, or trenches, to defend themselves. After this, neither side was able to advance very far, and the war dragged on for four years.

Soldiers lived in the trenches for weeks at a time. During a battle, they climbed out of the trench and charged at the enemy across an area known as No Man's Land. Millions of men died in these terrible battles that sometimes lasted for months.

This scene shows British soldiers in a trench on the Western Front.

A shell explodes in No Man's Land.

A soldier, called a sentry, keeps watch.

Machine gun

Boxes of machine-gun bullets

Officers live in underground shelters, called dug-outs.

Wooden walkways, called duckboards, stop the soldiers from sinking into the mud.

The trenches swarm with rats, flies, fleas and lice.

Poppies that grew on the battlefields of the Western Front became a symbol for remembering the war.

The war spreads

Other countries soon became involved in the war. Turkey and Bulgaria joined the Central Powers, while Italy, Greece and Portugal supported the Allies. The two sides also fought in Africa and the Far East, where Britain, Germany and other European countries had colonies.

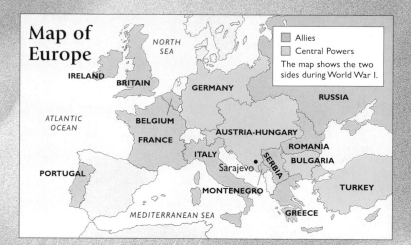

Map of Europe

Allies
Central Powers
The map shows the two sides during World War I.

NORTH SEA
IRELAND
BRITAIN
GERMANY
RUSSIA
ATLANTIC OCEAN
BELGIUM
FRANCE
AUSTRIA-HUNGARY
ITALY
ROMANIA
PORTUGAL
Sarajevo
SERBIA
BULGARIA
MONTENEGRO
TURKEY
GREECE
MEDITERRANEAN SEA

Ships and submarines

Both sides tried to stop their enemies from getting food and raw materials to make weapons. German submarines, called U-boats, sank any ship going to a British port. Some of these ships were American, and this provoked the USA into joining the war, in April 1917, on the side of the Allies.

The war ends

By March 1918, the Russians were exhausted by the war, and they made peace with Germany. German soldiers made a series of final attacks on the Western Front, but they were forced back. Germany surrendered, and on November 11, 1918, the war finally came to an end.

Walls supported by wooden planks

Barbed wire

Sandbags

This man has been sent some extra food by his family.

The men rest in holes dug into the sides of the trench.

The soldiers' feet are always wet and often get infected.

Important dates

June 1914 Archduke Franz Ferdinand is murdered.

July 1914 Austria-Hungary declares war on Serbia.

Sep 1914 The Germans are stopped by the Allies at the Battle of the Marne.

July-Nov 1916 Over a million soldiers die at the Battle of the Somme, in France.

April 1917 The USA joins the war.

March 1918 Russia makes peace with Germany.

Nov 11, 1918 The war ends.

THE WORLD

69

The Russian Revolution

At the start of the 20th century, Russia owned a vast empire that covered one sixth of the Earth's surface. Most of its people were peasants who lived in terrible poverty, but in the capital city of St. Petersburg, wealthy nobles lived a life of luxury.

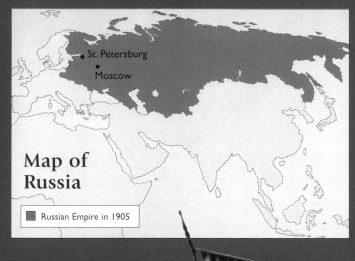

Map of Russia

■ Russian Empire in 1905

Tsar Nicholas II of Russia with his wife and family, photographed around 1900

Russia was ruled by a powerful emperor, or tsar, who believed he had been chosen by God. The tsar was advised by officials from noble families, but most Russians had no say in how their country was run.

Time for change

Many Russians were unhappy that the tsar had so much power. Some wanted him to rule with the help of a parliament chosen by the people. Others wanted a revolution to get rid of the tsar altogether. One group of revolutionaries were the Bolsheviks, led by Vladimir Ilyich Ulyanov, better known as Lenin.

The Bolshevik leader Lenin

The 1905 Revolution

In January 1905, over 150,000 workers marched to the tsar's Winter Palace in St. Petersburg to protest about their dreadful working conditions. The army fired on the protesters, killing over a hundred people. Workers across Russia went on strike, and Tsar Nicholas was forced to set up a parliament. But he made sure it had very little power.

Russia at war

In 1914, Russia entered the First World War (see pages 68 and 69). The Russian army suffered terrible defeats, losing over a million men in the first six months. At home, the war caused shortages of food, and people began to starve. Many Russians blamed the tsar for all these problems.

Revolution!

By March 1917, St. Petersburg (which had been renamed Petrograd) was running out of bread. Riots broke out and workers went on strike. When the army joined in the riots, Tsar Nicholas realized he had lost control and gave up the throne.

A temporary government was set up, but it did nothing to solve Russia's problems and soon became unpopular. In November 1917, the Bolsheviks, led by Lenin, seized power and took control of the country.

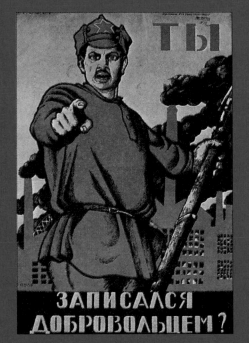

These Russian soldiers are joining the Revolution in March 1917. One of them is holding a red flag, which was a symbol of the Revolution.

Civil war

Lenin made peace with Germany and took Russia out of the First World War. He moved the capital to Moscow, gave land to the peasants and put workers in charge of the factories. Many wealthy Russians didn't like these changes, and this led to a bitter civil war between the Bolsheviks (now known as Communists) and their enemies. In 1918, Tsar Nicholas and his family were killed by a group of Communists.

A civil war poster urging people to join the Communist fighting force, known as the Red Army

Communist control

By 1921, the Communists had won the civil war, and Lenin was in complete control of Russia. He began the massive task of rebuilding the country, which was in chaos after years of fighting. In 1922, Russia was renamed the Union of Soviet Socialist Republics (USSR), also known as the Soviet Union.

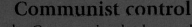

Important dates

1894	Nicholas II becomes Tsar of Russia.
January 1905	Soldiers fire on protesters in St. Petersburg.
1914	The First World War begins.
March 1917	Riots break out in Petrograd. The tsar gives up his throne.
Nov 1917	The Bolsheviks seize power.
1918-1921	Civil war in Russia
May 1918	Tsar Nicholas II and his family are shot.
Dec 1922	Russia is renamed the USSR.

Stalin's Soviet Union

After the Russian Revolution, the Communist leader Lenin was seen as a hero by many Russians. But Lenin did not rule the new Soviet Union for long. From 1922, he was often unwell, and he died in 1924.

Josef Stalin in military uniform

After Lenin's death, several leading Communists struggled for power. One of these men was Josef Stalin, the Secretary of the Communist Party. Stalin had many friends in the Party, and he used them to get rid of his rivals. By 1928, Stalin had complete control of the country.

Factories and workers

Stalin launched a Five Year Plan to turn the Soviet Union into a modern, industrial country. He forced people to leave their villages and work in factories in the city. Factories were expected to produce much more than before, and workers who didn't work fast enough were punished like criminals.

A Soviet poster urging workers to carry out the Five Year Plan

Farms and peasants

To keep the factory workers well fed, Stalin needed to reorganize farming. Peasant farmers were told to give up their tiny strips of land, and these strips were then joined together to create vast farms, called collective farms. The peasants were paid to work on the farms, and the crops they grew were sold to the government at a low price.

This statue of a factory worker and a peasant woman makes the Soviet way of life look heroic.

The worker holds a hammer, while the peasant woman has a farm tool called a sickle.

Kulaks and camps

Some peasants, known as kulaks, owned their own land, and when they refused to give it up Stalin used force. Millions of kulaks were arrested and sent to live in remote parts of the Soviet Union. There, they had to work in harsh prison camps, where many of them died of cold, hunger and exhaustion.

These Soviet farmers are carrying a banner which says that they will destroy the kulaks.

Many peasants destroyed their crops and killed their animals rather than hand them over to the collective farms. This meant that there was a terrible shortage of food, and millions of people died of hunger.

Removing enemies

By 1934, Stalin was worried that his enemies were plotting against him, so he decided to get rid of them. Anyone who criticized him was arrested by the secret police and executed, or sent to a prison camp. As many as 24 million people may have died in these brutal attacks, known as purges.

War and after

In 1941, during the Second World War, the Soviet Union was invaded by Germany. After many fierce battles, the Soviet army drove the Germans back across eastern Europe. Stalin used this success to turn the Soviet Union into a great world power (see page 88).

Counting the cost

Under Stalin, the Soviet Union became a strong, industrial country with factories, steel works, power stations and railways. Lots of new hospitals were built, and all children were given a free education. But Stalin was a ruthless leader. By the time he died, he had caused the deaths of as many as 40 million Soviet people.

The worker's hammer and the peasant's sickle became part of the symbol of the Soviet Union.

Important dates

1924	Lenin dies.
1928	Stalin begins a Five Year Plan to modernize industry and farming.
1929	Collective farms are set up.
1932-1933	Millions die in a terrible famine.
1934	The purges begin.
1941-45	The Soviet Union is at war with Germany.
1953	Stalin dies.

EUROPE

73

The People's Republic

Since 1644, China had been ruled by a family of powerful emperors called the Manchus. By 1900, the Manchus were very unpopular, but they refused to change the way the country was run.

In 1911, a revolution broke out. A group of nationalists, called the Kuomintang, seized power and set up a republic. The Kuomintang leaders found it hard to bring the country under control, but by 1928 they governed most of China.

Not everyone supported the Kuomintang. The Chinese Communist Party wanted China to be run by the workers and peasants, rather than by the rich. One group of Communists, led by Mao Zedong, set up their own government in Jiangxi (say "jang-shee"), in the south.

The Long March

In 1934, the Communists in Jiangxi were surrounded and attacked by the Kuomintang army. The Communists escaped and set off to find a safe place far away from the Kuomintang. This famous journey, which covered a distance of 8,000km (5,000 miles), is known as the Long March. Out of 100,000 people who set out on the march, 70,000 died on the way.

The marchers are trudging down a rocky mountain path.

The men are wearing the uniform of the Communist Red Army.

This picture shows Communists on the Long March. Most of the men have had to leave their wives and children behind.

During the Long March, the Communists had to cross 18 mountain ranges, including these mountains in Sichuan, in western China.

Map of China

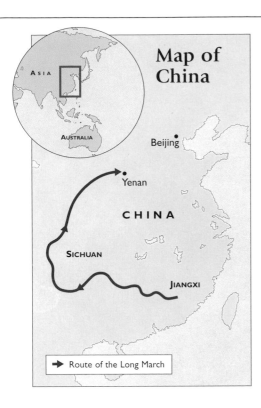

ASIA

AUSTRALIA

Beijing

Yenan

CHINA

SICHUAN

JIANGXI

→ Route of the Long March

Mao Zedong, leader
of the Chinese
Communist Party
from 1935 to 1976

Communist China

Between 1937 and 1945, China was at war with Japan. After the war, the struggle between the Communist Party and the Kuomintang continued. In 1949, the Communists, led by Mao Zedong, defeated the Kuomintang. Mao set up the People's Republic of China and took control of the country.

The Great Leap Forward

In 1958, Mao started a campaign, known as the Great Leap Forward, to try to build up industry. Many peasants were taken away from farms to work in factories. This meant that not enough crops were planted, and millions of people died of hunger.

The Cultural Revolution

Mao became worried that China was moving away from true Communism. In 1966, he started a new campaign, called the Cultural Revolution. He encouraged young people to attack traditional ideas and to criticize their teachers, bosses and parents.

Schools and universities were closed, and educated people were forced to work on the land. Groups of teenagers, known as Red Guards, beat and tortured anyone they thought was against the Revolution.

A young Chinese Red Guard

After three years of chaos, the army was sent in to stop the violence. The Cultural Revolution finally came to an end when Mao died in 1976.

Important dates

1911	The Kuomintang starts a revolution in China.
1912	The Kuomintang sets up a republic.
1934-1935	The Long March
1949	Mao Zedong sets up the People's Republic of China.
1958-1960	The Great Leap Forward
1966	Mao Zedong starts the Cultural Revolution.
1976	Mao Zedong dies.

Good Times, Bad Times

During the 1920s, the United States of America was the richest country in the world. Businesses boomed and factories produced lots of new goods, such as washing machines, vacuum cleaners and cars. Not everyone was rich, but most Americans thought life was getting better.

The Jazz Age

The 1920s are often known as the Jazz Age because of the new music and dances that were popular at that time. Some daring young women, known as flappers, cut their hair short and wore their skirts above the knee.

These two people are performing a popular 1920s jazz dance called the Charleston.

Banning alcohol

From 1920 to 1933, it was illegal to make or sell alcohol in the USA. This period of time is known as the Prohibition. Many people drank secretly in illegal bars, called speakeasies, and gangsters, such as Al Capone, grew rich by making, smuggling and selling alcohol.

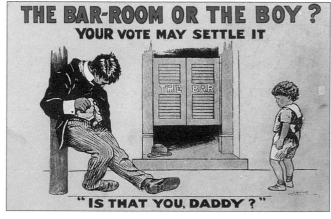

This 1920s postcard encourages Americans to vote for the banning of alcohol.

The Wall Street Crash

The good times came to an end in 1929, when thousands of people were ruined in a financial disaster known as the Wall Street Crash.

During the 1920s, many Americans had bought shares in businesses, hoping to make money by selling them later at a higher price. But in October 1929 share prices began to fall. People panicked and started selling their shares. This made prices drop even lower, until the shares were almost worthless.

This disaster is known as the Wall Street Crash because Wall Street is the home of the New York Stock Exchange, where shares are bought and sold.

The Great Depression

After the Wall Street Crash, banks and businesses failed, and millions of people lost their jobs. Thousands of families lost their homes as well, because they couldn't afford to pay the rent. This period of terrible poverty is known as the Great Depression. It lasted for most of the 1930s and affected countries all over the world.

Some homeless families had to live in shacks like this that they built out of cardboard.

The Dust Bowl

The Great Depression also affected farmers. In the USA, the situation was made worse by the weather. In some central areas, fierce winds blew away the dusty soil, making it impossible to grow crops. These areas became known as the Dust Bowl. Many farming families left their homes to look for work in California, on the west coast.

Here you can see a farm in the Dust Bowl being battered by a violent dust storm.

The New Deal

In 1932, Franklin D. Roosevelt became President of the USA. He started up a series of projects, known as the New Deal, to help industry and farming, and create new jobs. This did not end the Depression, but it made life easier for many Americans.

Important dates

1920-1933	The Prohibition
Oct 24, 1929	The Wall Street Crash
1932	Franklin D. Roosevelt becomes President.
1933	Roosevelt launches the New Deal.

NORTH AMERICA

The Rise of Fascism

After the First World War, many countries in Europe faced huge problems. Governments had very little money because they had spent so much on weapons for the war. Lots of people were out of work, and there wasn't enough food for everyone. People began to think that these problems needed drastic new solutions.

The first fascist

In Italy, the problems were particularly bad. Many people turned to Benito Mussolini, the leader of the Fascist Party. Mussolini became prime minister of Italy in 1922. Soon, he banned all other political parties and took complete control of the country. This way of ruling is known as fascism.

Mussolini salutes the crowd at a huge public meeting.

Germany defeated

After World War I, the winning countries decided that Germany should pay for the damage caused by the war. The Germans were forced to reduce the size of their army and navy, and were not allowed to have an air force. Germany also had to give up large areas of land. Many Germans felt angry and humiliated by all of this, and they blamed their government for agreeing to it.

The Depression

In 1929, Germany was hit by the Great Depression (see page 77). Millions of Germans lost their jobs, but the government did nothing to help. People became desperate, and some turned to the National Socialist Workers' Party (the Nazi Party), led by Adolf Hitler.

New hope

Hitler persuaded people that their problems were caused by foreigners, especially Jews. He believed that the Germans were superior to other races, and said he would make Germany powerful again. He promised strong leadership, jobs for everyone and an end to poverty.

Total power

The Nazis held huge meetings, or rallies, all over Germany to persuade people to vote for them. By 1932, they were the biggest party in the German Reichstag (parliament), and in 1933 Hitler became chancellor (head of the government). He then persuaded the Reichstag to give him complete control of the country.

This is the badge of the Nazi Party. The symbol in the middle is called a swastika.

Nazi Germany

Once Hitler was in power, he banned all political parties except the Nazi Party. He took control of all newspapers and radio, and forced schools and universities to teach Nazi ideas. Children had to join Nazi youth groups, and anyone who disagreed with the Nazis was arrested by the secret police, which was called the Gestapo.

In this photograph, the German leader Adolf Hitler (in the middle of the picture) is inspecting members of a Nazi organization called the SA.

Persecuting Jews

A Jewish boy and his family being driven out of their home by Nazi soldiers

The Nazis made life impossible for Jews. They weren't allowed to marry Germans, own land, do certain jobs, or even go out at night. Gangs of Nazi thugs attacked Jewish people, vandalized Jewish shops and burned synagogues.

Important dates

1919	Mussolini sets up the Fascist Party in Italy.
1922	Mussolini comes to power.
1929	The Great Depression begins.
1933	Hitler becomes chancellor of Germany.
1934	Hitler takes complete control as *Führer* (leader) of Germany.
Nov 9, 1938	On *Kristallnacht* (the Night of Broken Glass) Nazis attack thousands of Jewish homes, shops and synagogues.

EUROPE

79

Europe at War

By 1934, the Nazi leader Adolf Hitler had complete control of Germany (see pages 78 and 79). Hitler planned to create a powerful empire made up of all the German-speaking people in Europe. He began by taking over Austria in March 1938.

Hitler's next target was the German-speaking part of Czechoslovakia, known as the Sudetenland. Britain and France wanted to avoid another war with Germany, like the First World War, so they agreed to let Hitler have the Sudetenland. But he soon took over the rest of Czechoslovakia as well.

On September 1, 1939, Hitler invaded Poland. Britain and France had already agreed to help Poland if it was attacked, so two days later they declared war on Germany. Italy later joined the war on the German side. Together, Germany and Italy were known as the Axis Powers.

German troops with a machine gun

Europe under attack

Nothing much happened for the first six months of the war. Then, in April 1940, Hitler's troops began their attack. They used tanks and planes to advance at incredible speed. By June 1940, Hitler had taken over most of western Europe.

Escape by sea

As the Germans swept into northern France, many French and British soldiers were trapped near Dunkirk, on the north coast. The British organized a huge rescue, using small boats and yachts, as well as ships from their navy. In nine days, over 330,000 men were taken safely to Britain.

The Battle of Britain

Hitler planned to invade Britain, but he knew he needed to destroy the British Royal Air Force first. From August to October 1940, British and German planes fought a fierce battle in the skies over southern England. The British had fewer planes, but still managed to win. After this defeat, Hitler gave up the idea of invading Britain.

Map of Europe

NORWAY

DENMARK

GREAT BRITAIN

GERMANY • Berlin

Dunkirk • Dresden • POLAND

SUDETENLAND

FRANCE

CZECHOSLOVAKIA

AUSTRIA

ITALY ALBANIA

Moscow •

SOVIET UNION

Stalingrad •

NORTH AFRICA

LIBYA El Alamein

- ■ Axis Powers
- □ Land occupied by Axis Powers in the 1930s
- ■ Land occupied by Axis Powers by June 1940

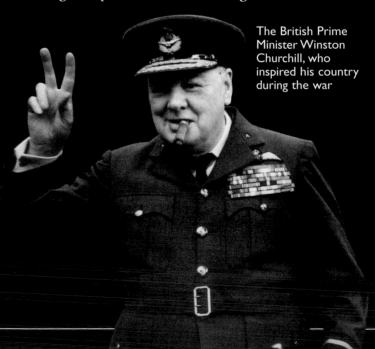

The British Prime Minister Winston Churchill, who inspired his country during the war

The Blitz

Hitler then tried to make the British surrender by bombing their cities. Night after night, German planes attacked, wrecking buildings and killing thousands of people. These attacks are known as the Blitz. The British fought back by bombing German cities, such as Dresden, where over 35,000 people were killed in one night.

This scene shows a typical London street during the Blitz. The bombing continued for nine months.

Powerful searchlights are used to spot German planes.

Anti-aircraft guns fire at the bombers.

Firefighters use water pumped from the river to fight the flames.

Thousands of British children were sent to live in the countryside, away from the bombing.

The Eastern Front

At the start of the war, the Germans and the Russians had agreed not to fight each other. But in June 1941, Hitler broke this agreement and invaded the Soviet Union. By December, the Germans had almost reached Moscow. But they weren't prepared for the freezing winter weather, and the Russians managed to drive them back.

This building has been hit by a fire bomb.

Hundreds of families have lost their homes.

This bus was thrown into the air by an exploding bomb.

Rescue workers dig survivors out of the rubble.

The bombs have made huge holes, or craters, in the street.

Gas and water pipes have been shattered.

This unexploded bomb could blow up at any minute.

The World at War

At first, the war against Hitler was fought mainly in Europe. The USA supported Britain and the Soviet Union by sending them weapons and tanks, but the US government didn't want to get involved in the fighting.

All this changed on December 7, 1941, when ships from the US navy were bombed by Japanese planes, at Pearl Harbor in Hawaii. The next day, the USA declared war on Japan. Hitler had signed an agreement with the Japanese, so he then declared war on the USA.

US battleships on fire after the Japanese attack on Pearl Harbor

War in the Pacific

The Japanese already controlled parts of China, which they had invaded in 1937. Determined to build up a new Japanese empire, they now advanced with frightening speed. By June 1942, Japan had taken over most of Southeast Asia and many of the islands in the Pacific Ocean (see map).

The Allies advance

The countries that fought against Japan and Germany were known as the Allies. From June 1942, the Allies began to push the Japanese back across the Pacific. They also won important battles in other parts of the world, such as El Alamein in North Africa and Stalingrad in the Soviet Union.

D-Day

On June 6, 1944, known as D-Day, the Allies made a surprise attack on the Germans in northern France. Thousands of Allied soldiers crossed the English Channel and landed on the beaches of Normandy. Slowly, they fought their way across France, reaching Germany in September 1944.

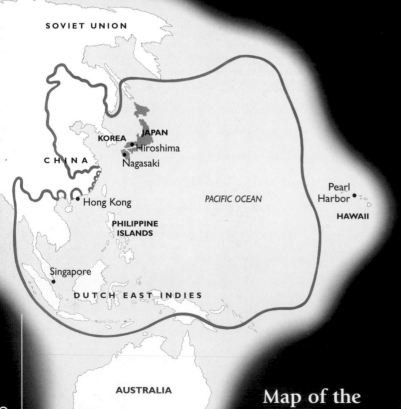

SOVIET UNION

KOREA
JAPAN
Hiroshima
CHINA
Nagasaki

Hong Kong

PACIFIC OCEAN

Pearl
Harbor

HAWAII

PHILIPPINE
ISLANDS

Singapore

DUTCH EAST INDIES

AUSTRALIA

Map of the Pacific

Japan
Area controlled by
Japan by 1942

This photograph, taken on D-Day, shows US soldiers wading from their landing craft onto one of the Normandy beaches.

Victory in Europe

Meanwhile, Russian troops were advancing into Germany from the east. In April 1945, they reached the capital, Berlin. Hitler realized he was defeated and killed himself on April 30. The Germans finally surrendered on May 8, known as V-E Day. (V-E stands for "Victory in Europe".)

The Holocaust

As the Allies advanced across Europe, they found prisons, or concentration camps, where the Nazis had sent Jews, gypsies and the mentally ill. Many of these people had been murdered by the Nazis. As many as 15 million people may have died in this way. This terrible event is known as the Holocaust.

The war ends

Although the war in Europe was over, fighting continued in the Pacific. On August 6, 1945, the USA dropped the first ever atomic bomb on the Japanese city of Hiroshima. About 80,000 people died in the explosion. Three days later, another bomb destroyed the city of Nagasaki, and the Japanese surrendered.

Atomic bombs, like the ones that destroyed Hiroshima and Nagasaki, form a huge, mushroom-shaped cloud when they explode.

Important dates

Sep 3, 1939	Britain and France declare war on Germany.
April-June 1940	Hitler occupies most of western Europe.
Aug-Oct 1940	The Battle of Britain
June 22, 1941	Hitler invades the Soviet Union.
Dec 7, 1941	Japan attacks US ships at Pearl Harbor.
June 6, 1944	The Allies land in France (D-Day).
April 30, 1945	Hitler kills himself.
May 8, 1945	Germany surrenders.
Aug 6, 1945	Hiroshima is destroyed by an atomic bomb.
Aug 14, 1945	The war ends.

THE WORLD

From Colonies to Countries

Since the 19th century, all of India and most of Africa had been ruled by Europeans. But by 1945, Europe had been weakened by the Second World War. The people of India and Africa at last saw their chance to break free and govern themselves. At the same time, some Europeans began to think it was time for the countries of Europe to give up their colonies.

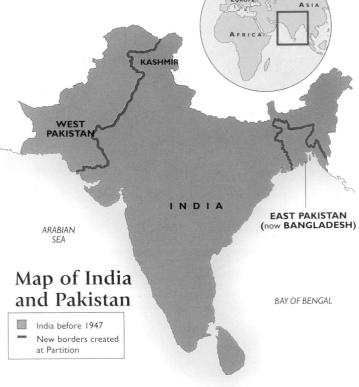

Map of India and Pakistan

KASHMIR

WEST PAKISTAN

INDIA

ARABIAN SEA

EAST PAKISTAN (now BANGLADESH)

BAY OF BENGAL

- India before 1947
- New borders created at Partition

Gandhi and India

A group called the Indian National Congress had fought against British rule in India since the 1880s. This group became much stronger in 1920, when a Hindu lawyer named Mohandas Gandhi took over as leader. Gandhi led many protests against the British, and although he protested peacefully he was often thrown into prison.

Gandhi was an inspiring leader and he became known as Mahatma, which means "Great Soul".

The British give in

During the Second World War, thousands of Indians fought on the British side and this helped to change Britain's attitude to India. In 1942, Britain promised that it would grant India its freedom after the war, provided that the Indians continued to help the British.

Two religions

Although most Indians wanted independence, fierce arguments broke out between Hindus and Muslims. They clashed because the Muslims did not want to be ruled by Hindus after India had become independent.

Two countries

On August 15, 1947, India became independent, but the day before this happened, it was divided into two separate countries. The mainly Hindu areas became present-day India, and the mainly Muslim areas became Pakistan. This division into two countries was called Partition.

Partition happened very fast, and riots broke out when people found themselves trapped in the "wrong" country. In 1999, arguments were still going on between India and Pakistan over areas of land such as Kashmir.

This photograph, taken in 1999, shows Indian soldiers celebrating a victory over Pakistani troops in Kashmir. The soldiers are holding up the Indian flag.

African independence

Until the 1950s, most of Africa was divided into colonies ruled by European countries (see page 56). This began to change in 1951 when Libya became the first African country to win its independence.

This is Jomo Kenyatta, a leading fighter for independence in Kenya and first president of his country.

Over the next 30 years, more than 40 African countries became independent. In some countries, such as Kenya and Mozambique, rebel soldiers known as guerrillas fought savage wars against their European rulers. These struggles for independence often lasted many years, but most of them were successful in the end.

White rebels

In parts of southern Africa, power was seized by white Europeans who had settled there. The British governor of Rhodesia, Ian Smith, declared his country's independence in 1965. Britain did not support Smith, and eventually the Africans took control. In 1980, Rhodesia became an independent African country and was renamed Zimbabwe.

Civil wars

After breaking free from European rule, many African countries still faced huge problems. Civil wars broke out in countries such as Nigeria, Angola, Chad and Somalia when people from different tribes or religions fought each other for power. Today, wars are still being fought in many parts of Africa.

Civil wars in Africa often force people to escape to nearby countries as refugees. These people are refugees from the civil war in Rwanda in 1995.

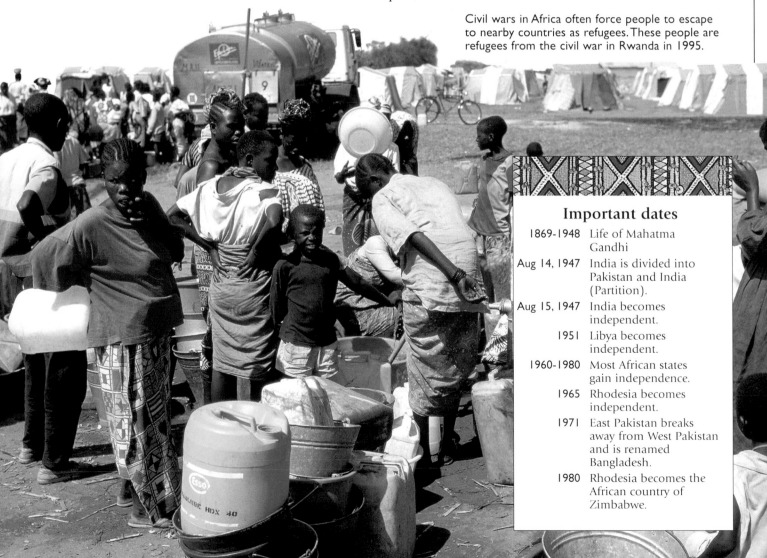

Important dates

1869-1948	Life of Mahatma Gandhi
Aug 14, 1947	India is divided into Pakistan and India (Partition).
Aug 15, 1947	India becomes independent.
1951	Libya becomes independent.
1960-1980	Most African states gain independence.
1965	Rhodesia becomes independent.
1971	East Pakistan breaks away from West Pakistan and is renamed Bangladesh.
1980	Rhodesia becomes the African country of Zimbabwe.

THE WORLD

85

War in the Middle East

The Middle East is the area around the Red Sea and the Persian Gulf. Since 1945, there have been many changes, invasions and wars in this troubled part of the world.

A Jewish homeland

In 1945, the country that is now Israel was called Palestine. It was controlled by British troops, but most of the people living there were Muslim Arabs, called Palestinians. However, Jews all over the world saw Palestine as their home, because the Jewish people had originally come from there.

Israel is born

During the Second World War, Jews in Europe were brutally persecuted by the Nazis, but some of them managed to escape to Palestine. After the war, an organization called the United Nations was set up to encourage peace and understanding between nations. The United Nations decided that the Jews should have a country of their own, and on May 14, 1948, the Jewish state of Israel was created in Palestine.

The Arabs attack

The creation of the new Jewish state infuriated the Palestinians, who were supported by other Arab countries, such as Egypt, Jordan and Syria. In May 1948, the Arab countries attacked Israel, but the Israelis fought back. By January 1949, Israel had won the war and thousands of Palestinians had fled from Israel. Those who stayed behind were not given the same rights as the Israelis.

The fighting continues

Over the next 20 years, the Arabs often attacked Israel's borders. These attacks increased after 1964 when the Palestine Liberation Organization (PLO) was formed to fight for the right of all Palestinians to live in Israel.

During the 1960s, many Palestinians, like these, were forced to leave their homes to escape the fierce fighting.

In 1967, Israeli troops seized large areas of Arab land in the dramatic Six-Day War, and in 1973 Egypt and Syria led a surprise attack on Israel in the Yom Kippur War. This period of fighting ended in 1979 when the Egyptian and Israeli leaders signed an agreement at Camp David in the USA.

Peace plans

During the 1990s, there were several attempts to make peace over Israel, and in 1993 Israel and the PLO agreed that some groups of Palestinians could have their own governments within Israel. However, in the last years of the 20th century, there were frequent clashes between the Israelis and the Palestinians who were living in Israel.

Israeli leader Yitzhak Rabin (on the left) and PLO leader Yasser Arafat shake hands during the 1993 Middle East peace talks, while US President Bill Clinton looks on.

Revolution in Iran

For most of the 20th century, Iran was ruled by a series of kings, or shahs. The last shah tried to modernize his country, but he was opposed by strict Muslims who wanted to keep the old traditions. In 1979, the Shah was overthrown and Ayatollah Khomeini, a Muslim leader, took control of Iran. The Ayatollah ruled Iran very strictly and ordered all Iranian women to wear traditional dress.

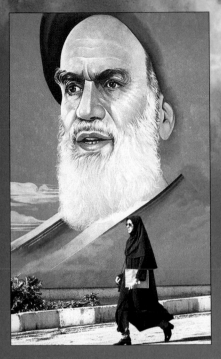

Here, a young Iranian woman in traditional dress is walking past a gigantic portrait of Ayatollah Khomeini.

Map of the Middle East

IRAN

EUROPE · ASIA

AFRICA

SYRIA

LEBANON

IRAQ

ISRAEL

JORDAN

KUWAIT

EGYPT

PERSIAN GULF

SAUDI ARABIA

RED SEA

☐ Areas claimed by Israel but occupied by Palestinians

The Gulf War

In 1990, Iraq invaded nearby Kuwait, hoping to gain control of Kuwait's oil wells. This led to the Gulf War, which started in 1991. A group of countries led by the USA and Saudi Arabia, attacked Iraq to force it to free Kuwait. After just two months, Iraq lost the war, but both Iraq and Kuwait had been badly damaged.

Oil wells like this were set on fire by Iraqi troops as they retreated from Kuwait at the end of the Gulf War.

The Iran-Iraq War

War broke out in 1980 between Iran and nearby Iraq. The war was really based on ancient differences between the two countries, but it began when Iraq invaded an area on Iran's border. The Iraqi leader, Saddam Hussein, thought Iran would be easy to beat, as it was in chaos after the revolution in 1979. In fact, the war dragged on for eight years and neither side won. By the time Iran and Iraq made peace in 1988, over a million soldiers had been killed.

Important dates

1948	Israel is created.
1964	Palestinians form the Palestine Liberation Organization (PLO).
1967	Six-Day War
1973	Yom Kippur War
1979	Revolution in Iran
1980-1988	Iran-Iraq War
1990	Iraq invades Kuwait.
1991	Gulf War
1993	Middle East Peace Accord between Israel and the PLO

The Cold War

During the Second World War, the USA and the Communist Soviet Union fought on the same side. But soon after the war, they became suspicious of each other. For the next 40 years, they fought a war of words and threats that became known as the Cold War.

Communism spreads

By the end of World War II, the Soviet Army had advanced across eastern Europe and into Germany. After the war, Soviet soldiers remained in eastern Europe, and the Soviet leader, Stalin, helped to set up Communist rulers there.

Taking sides

Western countries, such as the USA and Britain, grew worried that the Soviets wanted to control all of Europe. So, in 1949, these countries formed an organization called NATO (the North Atlantic Treaty Organization). All the members of NATO agreed to defend each other if the Soviets attacked.

In 1955, the Soviet Union and the Communist countries of eastern Europe made a similar agreement among themselves, called the Warsaw Pact.

Map of eastern Europe

SOVIET UNION

EAST GERMANY

Berlin

POLAND

WEST GERMANY

CZECHOSLOVAKIA

HUNGARY

ROMANIA

YUGOSLAVIA

BULGARIA

ALBANIA

■ Communist countries
— Iron Curtain

Germany divided

At the end of World War II, Germany was divided into four zones. The eastern zone was controlled by the Soviet Union, while the three western zones were run by the USA, Britain and France. In 1949, the Soviet zone became the Communist country of East Germany. The rest became West Germany.

The Berlin Wall

Berlin, the old capital city, now lay inside East Germany, and it too was divided into East and West. Life was much harder for people in East Berlin, and many of them tried to move to West Berlin. To stop this from happening, the Soviets built a huge wall between the two parts of the city. Any East Germans who tried to escape over the wall were shot.

This is part of the Berlin Wall, which became a symbol of the "Iron Curtain" that separated eastern Europe from the West.

East German flag

This is the Brandenburg Gate in East Berlin. It was built between 1788 and 1791 as a gateway into the city of Berlin.

West German police

THE WORLD

Crisis in Cuba

During the Cold War, both sides built up huge supplies of weapons. In 1962, the USA discovered that the Soviet government was planning to use the island of Cuba, near the American coast, as a base for its nuclear missiles. The situation became very tense, as neither side wanted a nuclear war. After six days, the Soviet government was persuaded to back down.

Wounded American soldiers being rescued by helicopter during the Vietnam War

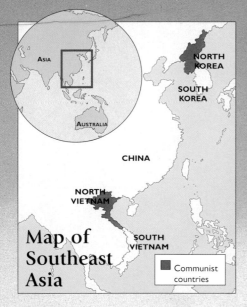

Map of Southeast Asia

Communist countries

NORTH KOREA
SOUTH KOREA
ASIA
AUSTRALIA
CHINA
NORTH VIETNAM
SOUTH VIETNAM

Korea and Vietnam

The USA and the Soviet Union never actually fought each other during the Cold War. But both sides sent weapons and troops to support Communists and anti-Communists who were fighting each other in different parts of the world. The main places where this happened were Korea and Vietnam.

Changing times

During the 1970s, the USA and the Soviet Union became more friendly. This changed when the Soviets invaded nearby Afghanistan in 1979, and the USA began planning powerful new weapons. In 1991, the Soviet Union split up, and the Cold War finally came to an end (see pages 92 and 93).

This sign near the Berlin Wall warns people that they are about to leave West Berlin.

East German guards

ACHTUNG!
Sie verlassen jetzt
WEST-BERLIN

Important dates

1945	World War II ends.
1949	NATO is formed. Germany becomes two separate countries.
1950-1953	The Korean War
1954-1973	The Vietnam War
1955	The Warsaw Pact is signed.
1961	The Berlin Wall is built.
1962	The Cuban Missile Crisis
1979	The Soviet Union invades Afghanistan.
1991	The Cold War ends.

THE WORLD

The Space Race

For hundreds of years, people dreamed of exploring space, but space travel only became possible when the rocket was invented in the 1930s. The first rockets were used during World War II to carry German bombs. After the war, scientists set about building a rocket powerful enough to travel into space.

Once the Cold War began in the 1950s, the USA and the Soviet Union competed fiercely to be the first country to send a rocket into space.

Satellites in space

In October 1957, the Soviets launched *Sputnik 1*. This was the first man-made object to go into space, and circle, or orbit, the Earth. Today, objects like this, called satellites, are used to take detailed photographs of the Earth and to send television pictures all around the world.

The photograph above was taken by a modern satellite orbiting the Earth. It shows the Sacramento River and the city of Sacramento, in California.

People in space

The Soviets scored another first in April 1961, when Yuri Gagarin became the first person to travel into space. During a flight that lasted 108 minutes, Gagarin made one complete orbit of the Earth. When he returned to the Soviet Union, he was treated as a hero.

Yuri Gagarin, photographed on the way to his spacecraft *Vostok 1*

Flying to the Moon

In the early 1960s, the Soviets were winning the space race and the Americans were desperate to change this. The US president, John F. Kennedy, announced a daring plan to put American astronauts on the Moon.

This is one of the giant *Saturn 5* rockets that were used to send American astronauts to the Moon.

In December 1968, an American spacecraft, *Apollo 8*, flew around the Moon for the first time. Six months later, US astronauts Neil Armstrong and Buzz Aldrin became the first people to set foot on the Moon.

Buzz Aldrin on the surface of the Moon on July 20, 1969

The space shuttle

The early manned spacecraft of the 1960s and 1970s could only be used once. Their crews returned to Earth by dropping out of the sky in a tiny capsule that had parachutes attached to it to help break its fall.

All this changed in 1981 when the American space shuttle flew for the first time. The shuttle takes off like a rocket, but lands on a runway, like a plane, so it can be used many times.

The space shuttle *Endeavour* blasting off from Cape Canaveral in the USA

Two rocket boosters help the shuttle reach a speed of 84km (54 miles) per minute.

USA

NASA
Endeavour

These wings help the shuttle glide back down to Earth.

At a height of 43km (27 miles), the boosters fall away. They drop into the sea and can be used again.

Space stations

During the 1970s, both the USA and the Soviet Union launched space stations, where scientists could live for weeks at a time and carry out experiments.

When the Cold War ended, the two countries began to work together. From 1995 to 1998, American scientists worked on the Russian space station *Mir*.

The space station *Mir*

At the end of the 20th century, engineers around the world started work on an exciting new project, called the International Space Station. The first two parts were built in Russia and in the USA. They were launched separately and were joined together in space, in December 1998.

Important dates

1957	*Sputnik 1*, the first satellite, is launched.
1961	Yuri Gagarin is the first person in space.
July 20, 1969	*Apollo 11* reaches the Moon. Neil Armstrong and Buzz Aldrin make the first Moon landing.
1971	The Soviets launch the world's first space station, *Salyut 1*.
1981	The space shuttle makes its first flight.
1986	The space shuttle *Challenger* explodes after lift-off, killing seven astronauts.
Dec 1998	The first two parts of the International Space Station link up.

THE WORLD

91

Rights for All

Human rights are based on the idea that all people should be treated fairly and equally, whatever their race, religion or sex. They should be able to live in freedom, express their opinions, have a fair trial and vote in elections. Today, these basic rights are often taken for granted, but a hundred years ago things were very different.

Votes for women

In 1900, most countries in the world did not allow women to vote in elections. New Zealand had given women the vote in 1893, but other countries were slow to follow. In Britain and the USA, women known as suffragettes campaigned fiercely for the right to vote. Britain finally gave women the vote in 1918, and the USA did the same two years later.

Many suffragettes, like this woman, were arrested and sent to prison.

Black rights

In the USA, during the 1950s, African-Americans began to protest at the way they were being treated. In many southern states, black people were prevented from voting and weren't allowed to send their children to white schools, or sit in bus seats reserved for whites.

This is Martin Luther King, a Baptist minister who led many black protests in the USA.

The largest protest took place in August 1963, when 200,000 people marched through the streets of Washington, DC. The next year, the US government passed new laws, making it illegal to treat people differently because of their race. In spite of this, even today, many black Americans do not have the same advantages as whites.

In some countries, such as China, people are not allowed to protest against the government. Here you can see Chinese students protesting in Beijing, in May 1989. Hundreds of them were killed when the army was sent in to stop the protests.

South Africa

Meanwhile, in South Africa, black Africans were treated appallingly by the whites who ruled the country. They weren't allowed to vote, and laws were passed to keep them out of white areas. This system of keeping blacks and whites apart was known as apartheid, and thousands of black Africans were jailed, beaten or killed for protesting against it.

In 1989, a new president, F. W. de Klerk, came to power and began changing the system. The following year, he released the black leader Nelson Mandela from prison. In 1994, black Africans were allowed to vote for the first time, and Nelson Mandela was chosen as South Africa's first black president.

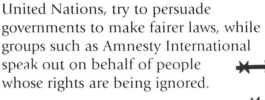

Nelson Mandela surrounded by supporters during the election campaign of 1994

The right to land

Many native people around the world have been treated unfairly by white settlers. In Australia, the native Aboriginals lost their land and their way of life when Europeans arrived in the 18th century. Since the 1930s, the Aboriginal people have been campaigning to win back their land, but so far they have only been given a tiny fraction of what they lost.

Protecting rights

Today, there are still many parts of the world where people's rights are not respected. In many countries, women are still seen as second-class citizens, and people are treated unjustly because of their race.

International organizations, such as the United Nations, try to persuade governments to make fairer laws, while groups such as Amnesty International speak out on behalf of people whose rights are being ignored.

This is the symbol of Amnesty International, which campaigns for people imprisoned for their beliefs.

Important dates

1893	Women in New Zealand are given the right to vote.
1945	The United Nations is set up to encourage peace and to protect human rights.
1949	Apartheid is introduced in South Africa.
1964-1965	Civil rights laws are passed in the USA.
1989	Hundreds of protesters are killed in Tiananmen Square in Beijing, China.
1990	Apartheid ends in South Africa.

Sound and Pictures

In 1900, radios and moving pictures, or movies, had only just been invented, and television did not exist at all. Over the next hundred years, these new inventions created a whole new area of entertainment and completely changed our view of the world.

The birth of cinema

In 1895, two brothers, named Louis and Auguste Lumière, invented a machine called a Cinématographe, which could project moving images onto a screen. The brothers gave their first movie show in Paris in December 1895, and cinema was born.

Moving pictures quickly became very popular, and the craze soon spread to the United States. By the 1920s, Hollywood, on the west coast of the USA, was the movie capital of the world.

© Disney Enterprises, Inc.

Mickey and Minnie Mouse were two very popular characters in early cartoon films.

The comic actor Charlie Chaplin was the most famous movie star of the 1920s.

The first talkie

Early moving pictures had no sound, but were accompanied by music from an orchestra or piano. The first major talking picture, or talkie, was *The Jazz Singer*, which was made in 1927.

Radio days

During the 1920s, radio also became popular. The first radio stations were set up in the United States in 1920, and by 1930 there were 12 million radio sets in the USA. Politicians soon realized that they could use radio to speak directly to people in their homes. During the Second World War, governments on both sides made radio broadcasts to encourage their own side and show the enemy in a bad light.

The start of television

The first public demonstration of a mechanical television was given by the British inventor John Logie Baird in 1926. The TV system we use today was developed in the 1930s, and in 1936 the BBC began regular TV broadcasts from London. At first, very few people had a TV set, as each one cost about the same as a small car. But by the 1950s, television was the most popular form of entertainment.

Satellite service

In 1962, for the first time, live TV pictures were sent across the Atlantic Ocean by a satellite orbiting the Earth. This meant that images filmed in the United States could be shown at the same time in Europe. Today, people can watch the news all over the globe as it happens, and our world seems a much smaller place.

This scene from *Lost in Space* shows a robot inside a space ship. The movie used a vast number of special effects to create a fantasy world in space.

Too much television?

By 1990, in the USA, the average teenager was spending 23 hours a week watching television. Some experts think that too much television makes people too lazy to think for themselves. Others worry that watching a lot of violence on television could make people behave in a violent way.

Movie magic

In order to compete with television, movie-makers had to create more spectacular effects. In the 1950s, new techniques were invented to improve sound and produce bigger, widescreen pictures. By the 1990s, movie companies were spending vast amounts of money on truly amazing special effects.

Important dates

1895 The Lumière brothers project moving images onto a screen.

1920 The first radio stations are set up in the USA.

1926 John Logie Baird demonstrates his television.

1927 *The Jazz Singer* is the first major movie with sound.

1936 The BBC begins regular television broadcasts.

1962 The satellite Telstar sends a TV image across the Atlantic.

THE WORLD

Our Polluted Planet

During the 20th century, daily life changed dramatically. We now have cars to take us from place to place, gas and electricity for cooking and heating, and a vast number of gadgets and machines to make life easier. But as early as the 1960s, scientists began to realize that our way of life was gradually destroying the world around us.

Global warming

Most of the world's electricity is produced in power stations that burn coal, oil or gas. When these fuels burn, they release a gas called carbon dioxide into the air. Exhaust fumes from cars and buses also contain carbon dioxide. Scientists now believe that this gas may be making the Earth warmer. This is known as global warming.

Trees use up some of the carbon dioxide in the air, helping to reduce global warming. But all over the world, forests like this are being burned to make room for farmland.

The greenhouse effect

As carbon dioxide rises high into the air, it forms a blanket around the Earth, trapping heat underneath. This is known as the greenhouse effect and it is what causes global warming. As the Earth warms up, the weather all over the world could change dramatically. Sea levels might also rise, flooding large areas of low-lying land.

Poisoning the air

Cars, factories and power stations continuously pump out fumes which dirty, or pollute, the air. In cities, these fumes sometimes form a smoky fog, called smog, which makes it hard for people to breathe. The fumes also mix with clouds to form acid rain which kills plants.

The ozone hole

The Earth is surrounded by a layer of gas called ozone, which blocks out harmful ultraviolet light from the Sun. In 1985, scientists showed that there was a hole in the ozone layer above Antarctica. We now know that the ozone layer is getting thinner in other parts of the world too.

The ozone is being destroyed by man-made gases called chlorofluorocarbons, or CFCs, which are found in some aerosols and refrigerators. As the ozone layer gets thinner, more ultraviolet light gets through, and this can damage our eyes and skin.

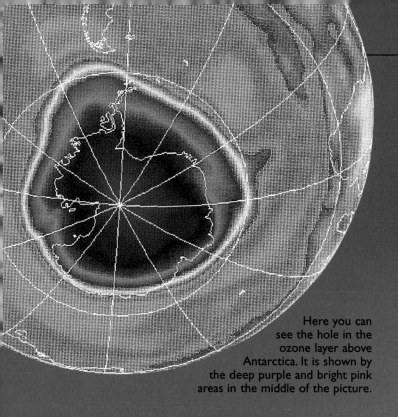

Here you can see the hole in the ozone layer above Antarctica. It is shown by the deep purple and bright pink areas in the middle of the picture.

Plastic pollution

Plastic is one of the most common materials around today. Because it is cheap, it is often used to make bags, bottles and wrappers which people throw away. Plastic doesn't rot, so it's very hard to get rid of. Lots of it ends up in the sea, where it kills millions of fish, birds and animals every year.

Turtles can die from eating plastic bags, which look like jellyfish in the water.

Saving the planet

Protest groups, such as Greenpeace, try to persuade governments to do something about pollution, and most world leaders now accept that there is a real problem. In 1992, politicians from over 150 countries met at the Earth Summit in Brazil to talk about the future of the planet.

In order to protect the ozone layer, a total of 140 countries have now agreed to stop making CFCs, and some countries have also agreed to cut the amount of carbon dioxide they produce. Scientists hope that this will help to slow down global warming.

One way to reduce global warming is to find cleaner ways of making electricity. These are wind turbines, which can produce electricity without releasing carbon dioxide into the air.

Polluting the water

The world's seas and rivers are being polluted by sewage (waste from drains and toilets) and poisonous chemicals dumped from factories. Our seas and rivers are also being poisoned by fertilizers that are washed off farmland. All around the world, beaches are ruined and seabirds are killed when oil leaks out of tankers that have run aground.

Important dates

1967	Scientists first become aware of the greenhouse effect.
1971	Greenpeace is set up.
1985	Scientists measure the hole in the ozone layer.
1992	The Earth Summit is held in Rio de Janeiro, in Brazil.

THE WORLD

The Computer Revolution

Computers allow us to do things that people used to think were impossible. We can test cars and planes before they are even built, explore imaginary worlds using virtual reality, and send information around the world in seconds on the Internet. Today, computer technology is changing incredibly fast, but progress was slow at first.

The first computers

The very first computers were invented in the 19th century. They made calculations mechanically, using lots of connected cogs and wheels. The first electronic computers did not appear until the 1940s, over a hundred years later. These early computers were immense. ENIAC, completed in 1946, filled a whole room and weighed as much as 500 people.

From valves to chips

Computers use electrical signals to process, or work on, information. Early computers, such as ENIAC, had thousands of large valves which switched on and off to produce these signals. Then, in 1947, a much smaller switch, called a transistor, was invented. Computers no longer needed to be quite so huge.

In 1958, an American scientist named Jack Kilby invented the microchip, which contained more than one transistor. By using microchips, it was possible to build computers that were much smaller and more powerful than before.

Today, microchips, like the one shown above, can contain millions of tiny transistors.

Personal computers

The first small home computer, the Altair, was sold in 1975. It was named after a planet in the TV series *Star Trek*. The Altair had to be bought as a kit and then built at home. Most modern computers are based on a type of computer called a PC that was first made in 1981.

The Internet

The Internet is a huge network that links together millions of computers all around the world. It grew out of a network called ARPANET, which was set up in 1969 by the US armed forces. At first, computers had to be connected to the Internet by special cables. It wasn't until the 1990s that people could link up by using their own phone line.

Here are some pages from the part of the Internet known as the World Wide Web.

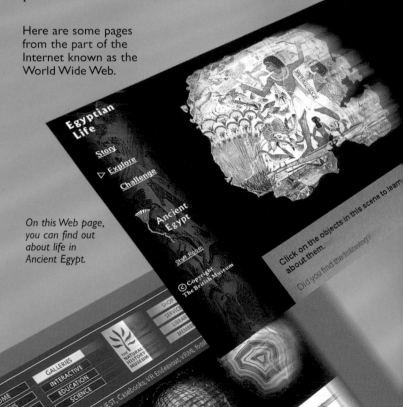

On this Web page, you can find out about life in Ancient Egypt.

Starting at this Web page, you can go on a tour around a museum.

The World Wide Web

Using the Internet, we can send electronic messages, or e-mail, around the world in seconds and find information on any topic we want, by searching the pages of the World Wide Web. Lots of people now shop on the Internet, buying anything from groceries to plane tickets.

Living with computers

Computers have had a huge effect on the way we live. Today, many people work from home, using a computer to connect to their workplace. Other jobs, such as assembling cars, can be done by computers instead of people. Many of the gadgets in our homes, such as washing machines and CD players, rely on tiny computers to make them work.

Okay, let's begin!

Back to Fun Online

Back to The Children's Museum

Using this page, you can create your own puppet show.

A Gutsy View

This page lets you see inside the human body.

This page gives you an up-to-date weather forecast.

Just for fun

The first popular electronic game, a simple tennis game called Pong, appeared in 1972. Today's computer games are much more complicated, with realistic images and dramatic sound effects. Computers are also used to create the amazing special effects you see at the movies. These techniques are now so good that it's impossible to tell what's real and what isn't.

This is a character from the 1995 movie Toy Story, which was the first full-length movie to be made entirely on computer.

Important dates

1834-1871	Charles Babbage designs the first mechanical computer.
1946	The ENIAC computer is completed.
1947	The transistor is invented.
1958	Jack Kilby makes the first microchip.
1969	The computer network ARPANET is set up.
1975	The first small home computer is sold.
1981	The first PC is made by the American firm IBM.
1989	British scientist Tim Berners-Lee invents the World Wide Web.

The End of the Century

The end of the 20th century was an exciting time, as new discoveries and inventions changed people's lives faster than ever before. At the same time, several parts of the world were devastated by terrible wars.

Yugoslavia breaks up

At the start of the 1990s, the country of Yugoslavia, in eastern Europe, split into separate republics. The largest of these republics, Serbia, wanted Yugoslavia to remain a single country, and war soon broke out between Serbia and the other republics. Fighting was especially violent in the republic of Bosnia-Herzegovina and in Kosovo, in southern Serbia.

The Serbs wanted to drive all non-Serbs out of Yugoslavia. This photograph shows refugees escaping from Kosovo.

East Timor breaks free

In August 1999, violence broke out in East Timor, in Southeast Asia. For more than 20 years, East Timor had been ruled by Indonesia, and when the East Timorese voted to become independent, Indonesian soldiers began attacking them.
The United Nations (UN) sent troops to protect the people of East Timor, and Indonesia soon agreed to let East Timor govern itself. UN soldiers stayed there to make sure the area remained peaceful.

The symbol of the UN

New technology

By the 1990s, advances in technology were changing the way many people lived and worked. New satellite phones allowed people to talk to each other from very remote places. More and more people used their computers to connect to the Internet, and a whole new industry grew up, as companies began using the Internet to sell things directly to people in their homes.

Understanding genes

By the end of the century, scientists had built up a vast amount of knowledge about human genes, the coded chemical messages that are passed on from parents to children. In 1990, a project was set up to discover how each gene in the body works. This is known as the Human Genome Project, and scientists hope that it will help them find cures for many diseases.

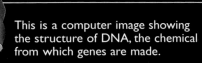

This is a computer image showing the structure of DNA, the chemical from which genes are made.

GM food

In the 1990s, scientists discovered how to transfer genes from one type of plant or animal to another. They used this knowledge to create crops that were protected against insects and diseases. Food from these crops is known as genetically modified, or GM, food. Although GM crops could help to provide enough food for everyone in the world, many people are afraid that they could also damage the environment.

The year 2000

The century ended with a bang as many countries held spectacular firework displays to celebrate the start of the year 2000. For the first time ever, television made it possible to watch people celebrating the dawn of a new century in different places all over the world.

Fireworks exploding in Paris at midnight on December 31, 1999

THE WORLD

World Time Chart

This chart shows what was happening at the same time in different parts of the world.

DATE	THE AMERICAS	EUROPE	AFRICA
1500	1500s Portuguese settlers arrive in Brazil. 1519-1521 Spanish conquistadors conquer the Aztecs. 1532-1534 Spanish conquistadors conquer the Incas. Inca priest 1580s The Slave Trade begins.	1520s The Reformation begins. 1545 The Counter-Reformation begins. 1547-1584 Ivan the Terrible is Tsar of Russia. 1556 Charles V divides the Habsburg Empire in two. Flag of the Habsburg Empire 1558-1603 Elizabeth I is Queen of England. 1581 The Republic of the United Netherlands is created.	1505 The Portuguese establish ports on the coast of East Africa. 1516-1560 The Ottoman Turks conquer large areas of North Africa.
1600	1603 French settlers start to set up colonies in Canada. 1620 The *Mayflower* arrives in North America carrying English pilgrims. 1699 The French create the colony of Louisiana.	1618-1648 The Thirty Years' War. 1630s Galileo proves that the Earth travels around the Sun. 1642-1646 The English Civil War. 1643-1715 Louis XIV is King of France. 1660s Isaac Newton discovers the laws of gravity. 1689-1725 Peter the Great is Tsar of Russia.	1616 Dutch and French traders set up trading posts in West Africa. 1652 Dutch settlers conquer Cape Colony.
1700	1759 British troops capture Quebec from the French. 1776 American colonists sign the Declaration of Independence. 1789 George Washington becomes the first President of the USA.	1740-1780 Maria Theresa rules the Habsburg Empire. 1740-1786 Frederick the Great is King of Prussia. 1750s The Industrial Revolution begins in Britain. 1762-1796 Catherine the Great is Tsarina of Russia. 1789 The French Revolution begins. Ribbons worn by French Revolutionaries 1799-1815 Napoleon Bonaparte rules France.	1700-1800 The African kingdoms of Benin, Oyo and Ashanti are flourishing. Ashanti gold ornament
1800	1816-1824 Simon Bolivar and José de San Martín win independence for colonies in South America. 1860 Abraham Lincoln becomes President of the USA. 1861-1865 The American Civil War. 1888 Slavery ends throughout the Americas. US President Abraham Lincoln	1848 Revolutions in many parts of Europe. 1861 Italy is unified. 1871 Germany is unified. 1895 Karl Benz, a German engineer, builds the first motor car. Benz's first motor car 1895 The Lumière brothers give the first ever movie show, in Paris.	1806 Britain takes control of Cape Colony. 1836 The Boers set out on the Great Trek. 1841 David Livingstone starts to explore Africa. 1879 The Zulus are defeated by the British and the Boers. 1899 The Boer War begins.

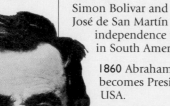

ASIA

AUSTRALASIA

THE MIDDLE EAST

1502 The start of the Safavid dynasty in Persia.

1520-1566 Sultan Suleiman rules the Ottomans.

Sultan Suleiman

1680s The Ottoman Empire begins to weaken.

Persian Safavid warriors

1730 The Safavid dynasty in Persia ends.

1854-1869 The Suez Canal is built in Egypt.

SOUTH ASIA

1526-1605 Babar is the first Mogul Emperor of India.

1556-1605 Akbar is the Mogul Emperor of India.

1600 The British East India Company is created.

1632 The Mogul Emperor Shah Jahan starts to build the Taj Mahal in India.

1690s The Mogul Empire is at its largest.

1714 Hindu princes start to win land in northern India.

1757 Robert Clive defeats the Prince of Bengal at the Battle of Plassey in India.

1857-1858 The Indian Mutiny.

1858 The British government takes control of India.

1885 The Indian National Congress is set up to campaign for independence.

Symbol of the Indian National Congress

THE FAR EAST

1568-1582 Oda Nobunaga controls Japan.

1591-1598 Toyotomi Hideyoshi controls Japan.

1595 Dutch traders start to set up colonies in the East Indies.

1603 The Tokugawa shoguns start to rule Japan.

1644 The Ming dynasty ends and the Manchu emperors take over China.

Ming jar

1839-1842 The Opium War in China.

1850-1864 The Taiping Rebellion in China.

1868 The Emperor takes control of Japan.

1894-1895 War between Japan and China.

1898-1900 The Boxer Rebellion in China.

Boxer warrior

Australian Aboriginal musical instruments, called clapsticks

1606 Dutch explorers reach Australia.

1642 Abel Tasman reaches New Zealand.

Australian kangaroo

1770 Captain Cook reaches Australia.

1788 Britain begins sending convicts to Australia.

1840 The British take control of New Zealand.

1860-1861 Explorers cross Australia.

1893 Women in New Zealand are given the right to vote.

DATE	THE AMERICAS	EUROPE	AFRICA

1900

THE AMERICAS

1914
Opening of
the Panama
Canal.

1917 The USA
joins World
War I.

1920 Prohibition
begins in the USA.

1927 *The Jazz Singer* is the
first major movie with
sound.

1929 The Wall Street Crash.

1933 US President Roosevelt
launches the New Deal.

1941 The USA joins World
War II after Pearl Harbor is
bombed.

EUROPE

1914-1918 World War I.

Poppies from the battlefields of
World War I

1917 The Russian Revolution.

1922 Benito Mussolini
takes control of Italy.

1928-1953 Josef Stalin
controls the Soviet Union.

Symbol of the
Soviet Union

1933 Adolf Hitler becomes
Chancellor of Germany.

1939-1945 World War II.

1948 Communists come to power
in Czechoslovakia, Hungary,
Romania, Bulgaria and Poland.

1949 Germany is divided into
East and West.

AFRICA

1902 The Boer War ends.

1942 The Allies defeat the
Germans at El Alamein in
North Africa.

1949 Apartheid is
introduced in South Africa.

1950

THE AMERICAS

1958 Jack Kilby invents the
microchip.

1962 The Cuban Missile
Crisis.

1963 US President
Kennedy is assassinated.

1968 Martin Luther King
is assassinated.

1969 US astronaut Neil
Armstrong is the first
man on the Moon.

US astronaut Buzz
Aldrin on the Moon,
photographed by Neil
Armstrong

1981 The US space
shuttle makes its
first flight.

1992 The Earth
Summit is held in
Rio de Janeiro,
Brazil.

EUROPE

1953 The structure of DNA is discovered in Britain by
Francis Crick and James Watson.

1957 The Soviet Union launches *Sputnik I* into space.

1961 Yuri Gagarin of the Soviet
Union is the first person in
space.

1980 Solidarity is set up in
Poland.

1985 Mikhail Gorbachev
becomes leader of the
Soviet Union.

1989 The Berlin Wall
falls.

1989 Tim
Berners-Lee invents
the World Wide Web.

1991 The Soviet Union
splits up.

1991-1995 War in
Yugoslavia.

1998-1999 War in
Kosovo.

AFRICA

1951 Libya becomes
independent.

1952-1955 Rebellion in
Kenya against British rule.

1957 Ghana becmes
independent.

1960-1980 Most African
states become
independent.

1967-1970 Civil war in
Nigeria.

Flag of South Africa

1990 Apartheid ends in
South Africa.

1994-1999 Nelson
Mandela is President of
South Africa.

2000

ASIA

AUSTRALASIA

THE MIDDLE EAST

SOUTH ASIA

THE FAR EAST

1904-1905 War between Japan and Russia.

1914-1918 Troops from Australia and New Zealand fight in World War I.

1918 The Turkish Ottoman Empire ends.

1910 Japan gains control of Korea.

1911 The Kuomintang start a revolution in China.

Mahatma Gandhi

1912 The last Manchu Emperor of China gives up his throne.

1922 The Republic of Turkey is formed.

1939-1945 Troops from Australia and New Zealand fight in World War II.

1920 Mahatma Gandhi starts a non-violent campaign for Indian independence.

1934 Communists in China set out on the Long March.

1941-1945 Japan fights the Allies in World War II.

1945 The first ever atomic bomb is dropped, on Hiroshima in Japan.

1948 Israel is created.

1947 India and Pakistan become independent.

1949 Mao Zedong sets up the People's Republic of China.

1948-1949 Arab-Israeli War.

1950-1953 The Korean War.

1956 Second Arab-Israeli War.

1967 Six-Day War between Israel and the Arab states.

1960 Mrs Bandaranaike of Ceylon is the first woman prime minister in the world.

1954 The Vietnam War starts.

1966 The Cultural Revolution in China.

A Chinese Red Guard from the time of the Cultural Revolution

Israeli fighter plane

1973 The Vietnam War ends.

1976 Death of Mao Zedong.

1973 Yom Kippur War between Israel and the Arab states.

1971 Bangladesh is formed.

1979 Ayatollah Khomeini takes control of Iran.

1980-1988 Iran-Iraq War.

1989 Hundreds of Chinese protesters are killed in Tiananmen Square.

1993 The Native Titles Bill gives some land rights to Aboriginals in Australia.

1990 Iraq invades Kuwait.

1991 The Gulf War.

Symbol of the UN

1993 Peace agreement between Israel and the Palestinians.

1999 UN soldiers are sent to East Timor to help it become an independent nation.

Word List

This list explains some of the words that are used in the book.

Aboriginals The native people who lived in Australia before the Europeans arrived.

allies People who fight on the same side in a war. During the two world wars, the countries that fought on the same side as Britain were known as the Allies.

apartheid The South African system of keeping different races of people apart. Apartheid lasted from 1949 to 1990, and meant that non-whites were treated as second-class citizens.

assassinate To murder a leader or a politician.

Axis Powers The countries that fought on the same side as Germany in the Second World War.

Bolshevik A Russian Communist who supported Lenin. The Bolsheviks led the revolution against the Tsar of Russia in 1917.

Catholic A person who belongs to a branch of the Christian Church which is led by the Pope in Rome.

Central Powers The countries that were on the same side as Germany in the First World War.

civil war Fighting between different groups of people within the same country.

Cold War The struggle for power between the United States and the Soviet Union, which was at its height during the 1950s and 1960s.

colonists People who set up a colony, or their descendants who live there.

colony A settlement created in a foreign land, by people who have moved away from their homeland.

Communism A form of government where the state owns all land and factories, and provides for people's needs. Today, China is the world's largest Communist country.

constitution A set of laws used to rule a country.

convict A person who has been found guilty of a crime and put in prison.

culture The shared ideas, beliefs and values of a group of people.

dynasty A series of rulers from the same family.

election The selection, by voting, of a person or a party to a position of power.

empire A large group of lands that is ruled by one powerful person.

famine A serious shortage of food which causes many people to die.

Fascism The military form of government in Italy from 1922 to 1943, led by Benito Mussolini, which banned all opposition. Fascism is also used to describe similar forms of government in other countries, such as Hitler's Germany.

Benito Mussolini, leader of the Italian Fascist Party

general A person who leads an army.

global warming The slow warming of the Earth's climate, which is caused by harmful gases from power stations, factories and car exhausts.

Great Depression The period of worldwide unemployment and poverty, which began after the Wall Street Crash of 1929 and lasted until the late 1930s.

Hindu A person who follows the Hindu faith, the main religion of India. Hindus pray to many gods and goddesses.

Holocaust The murder of six million Jews by German Nazis between 1940 and 1945.

Internet The vast computer network that links millions of computers around the world.

Iron Curtain A phrase used to describe the boundary that existed until 1989 between Western Europe and the Communist countries of Eastern Europe.

Jew A person who belongs to the race of people who are descended from the ancient tribes of Israel. The Jewish religion is based on the teachings of the Old Testament of the Bible.

Maoris The native people who lived in New Zealand before the Europeans arrived.

missionary A person who travels to a foreign country and tries to persuade the people living there to follow a different religion.

mosque A building where Muslims pray.

Muslim A person whose religion is based on the teachings of the Prophet Mohammed and on the holy book, the *Koran*.

nationalism The shared feeling among people who live in the same region and who have the same culture, language or religion. Nationalism often leads people to form their own independent nation.

NATO The North Atlantic Treaty Organization, an international organization which was set up in 1949 to defend Western countries against the Soviet Union. The USA, Canada and Britain are members of NATO.

Nazi Party The German National Socialist Workers' Party, led by Adolf Hitler who ruled Germany between 1933 and 1945. The Nazis were extremely anti-Jewish, and used force against anyone who opposed them.

noble A member of a family that belongs to the ruling class of a country.

parliament A group of people who meet to make decisions and create laws for their country.

peasant A person who works on the land.

pioneer A person who explores a new country or a new area of a country. Pioneers usually settle in the place they have explored.

plague A disease which spreads fast and kills many people.

plantation A large farm where crops such as cotton, coffee and tobacco are grown.

prime minister The leader of a government that has been chosen by the people.

Protestant A person who belongs to a branch of the Christian Church that started in western Europe in the 1500s. The Protestant Church does not have the Pope as its leader.

Puritan A person who belongs to a very strict Protestant branch of the Christian Church.

refugee A person who is forced to leave their homeland and live somewhere else. Refugees have usually escaped from wars or famines.

republic A country without a king or queen, whose leaders rule on behalf of the people.

revolution A successful rebellion by the people against a leader or a government.

satellite An object which circles the Earth in space. Man-made satellites can take photographs of the Earth, and are also used to send phone calls and television pictures from one part of the world to another.

scholar A person who studies, teaches, and writes books.

Soviet Union The Communist country that was formed in 1922 after the Russian Revolution. It was also known as the USSR.

state An area that has its own laws. A state can be an independent nation or part of a larger country.

strike A protest in which workers demand better pay or fairer working conditions by refusing to work.

suffragette A woman who campaigned for the right to vote at the end of the 19th and the beginning of the 20th century.

sultan A ruler of the Turkish Ottoman Empire or of other Muslim lands.

synagogue A building where Jews worship.

taxes Money collected from the people by a government or a ruler.

trade union An organization of workers who campaign together for better pay or fairer working conditions.

treaty An agreement between two or more countries.

tsar A Russian emperor.

tsarina A Russian empress.

UN The United Nations, an international organization which was set up in 1945 to encourage world peace.

the West The western part of the world which includes Europe and America. During the Cold War, the non-Communist countries of Europe and America were known as "the West".

World Wide Web A vast network of linked pages which are stored on computers around the world, providing information on a huge variety of subjects.

Index

Pages where you can find out most about a subject are shown in **bold** type.

Acknowledgements

Additional consultants: Stuart Atkinson, Chris Chandler, Dr. John Rostron & Dr. Margaret Rostron
Additional illustrations: Stephen Conlin, John Fox, Nicholas Hewetson, Simon Roulstone, Justine Torode & Ross Watton
Digital imaging: John Russell   Picture researcher: Ruth King   Artwork co-ordinator: Cathy Lowe
Additional contributions: Anna Claybourne

Every effort has been made to trace the copyright holders of material in this book. If any rights have been omitted, the publishers offer their sincere apologies and will rectify this in any subsequent editions, following notification. The publishers are grateful to the following individuals and organizations for their permission to reproduce material on the following pages (*t = top, m = middle, b = bottom, l = left, r = right*):

p4 *(bl)* ©Bettmann/CORBIS, *(br)* Digital image ©1996 CORBIS/Original image courtesy of NASA/CORBIS; **p5** *(tr)* ©Bettmann/CORBIS, *(br)* ©Bettmann/CORBIS; **p7** *(tr)* Sir Francis Drake, 1581 by Nicholas Hilliard/Kunsthistorisches Museum, Vienna, Austria/Bridgeman Art Library; **p8** ©Wolfgang Kaehler/CORBIS; **p10** *(bl)* The Art Archive, *(main)* ©Sheldan Collins/CORBIS; **p12** *(bl)* ©James L. Amos/CORBIS, *(t)* ©Bettmann/CORBIS, *(mr)* Mary Evans Picture Library; **p13** *(tl)* ©Gianni Dagli Orti/CORBIS, *(b)* ©Patrick Ward/CORBIS; **p14** ©Bettmann/CORBIS; **p16** *(tl)* ©Bettmann/CORBIS, *(b)* King Charles I of England out hunting, c.1635 by Sir Anthony van Dyck/Louvre, Paris, France/Giraudon/Bridgeman Art Library; **p17** ©WildCountry/CORBIS; **p18** *(bl)* ©Archivo Iconografico, S. A./CORBIS, *(r)* ©CORBIS; **p19** ©Archivo Iconografico, S. A./ CORBIS; **p21** *(tl)* ©Francis G. Mayer/CORBIS, *(tr)* Wageningen UR Library; **p22** ©Macduff Everton/CORBIS; **p23** *(t)* ©photo RMN/J. Derenne, *(m)* ©Archivo Iconografico, S. A./CORBIS; **p24** *(ml)* ©DigitalVision, *(bl)* The Anatomy Lesson of Dr. Nicolaes Tulp, 1632 (oil on canvas) by Rembrandt Harmensz van Rijn/Mauritshuis, The Hague, The Netherlands/Bridgeman Art Library; **p25** Science Museum/Science and Society Picture Library; **p26** ©Galen Rowell/CORBIS; **p27** *(b)* ©Archivo Iconografico, S. A./ CORBIS, *(tr)* NOVOSTI (London); **p28** ©Archivo Iconografico, S. A./CORBIS; **p29** The Art Archive; **p30** ©The Corcoran Gallery of Art/CORBIS; **p34** *(main)* ©Historical Picture Archive/CORBIS, *(t)* The Granger Collection, New York; **p35** US Library of Congress; **p38** National Trust Photographic Library/Erik Pelham; **p39** ©Hulton-Deutsch Collection/CORBIS; **p40** *(bl)* ©Philadelphia Museum of Art/CORBIS, *(tr)* Peter Newark's American Pictures; **p43** ©Archivo Iconografico, S. A./CORBIS; **p44** *(t)* ©Archivo Iconografico, S. A./CORBIS, *(b)* ©Archivo Iconografico, S. A./CORBIS; **p47** *(t)* The Art Archive, *(br)* National Museums & Galleries of Wales (Museum of Welsh Life); **p48** ©Robert Estall/CORBIS; **p49** ©Historical Picture Archive/CORBIS; **p51** *(m)* Hulton Getty, *(br)* Hulton Getty; **p52** *(mr)* ©Bettmann/CORBIS, *(b)* ©Gianni Dagli Orti/CORBIS; **p53** ©Gianni Dagli Orti/CORBIS; **p54** *(bl)* The Art Archive; **p55** *(tl)* The Art Archive, *(main)* ©Pablo Corral V/CORBIS; **p57** *(mt)* ©Hulton-Deutsch Collection/CORBIS, *(r)* ©Eric and David Hosking/CORBIS; **p58** *(bl)* Illustrated London News, *(m)* Illustrated London News; **p61** *(tl)* ©Bettmann/CORBIS, *(m)* ©Bettmann/CORBIS, *(b)* ©Dave G. Houser/CORBIS; **p62** ©Ric Ergenbright/CORBIS; **p64** The Art Archive; **p66** ©Michael S. Yamashita/CORBIS; **p67** *(t)* ©Underwood & Underwood/CORBIS, *(b)* ©Michael Holford; **p70** *(tl)* Illustrated London News, *(mb)* ©Brian Vikander/CORBIS; **p71** NOVOSTI (London); **p72** *(tl)* NOVOSTI (London), *(bl)* NOVOSTI (London), *(r)* ©Gregor Schmid/CORBIS; **p73** ©Bettmann/CORBIS; **p74** ©Tiziana and Gianni Baldizzone/CORBIS; **p75** AKG London; **p76** *(bl)* Archive Holdings, Inc./The Image Bank, *(tr)* Mary Evans Picture Library; **p77** *(tr)* ©CORBIS, *(br)* ©DigitalVision; **p78** *(main)* Hulton Getty, *(tr)* Hulton Getty; **p79** ©Hulton-Deutsch Collection/CORBIS; **p80** *(mt)* ©CORBIS, *(br)* Illustrated London News; **p81** ©Hulton-Deutsch Collection/CORBIS; **p82** ©Bettmann/CORBIS, *(b)* ©Bettmann/CORBIS; **p83** ©CORBIS; **p84** *(t)* Illustrated London News, *(b)* ©AFP/CORBIS; **p85** *(t)* ©Bettmann/CORBIS, *(b)* ©Howard Davies/CORBIS; **p86** *(tr)* ©Tim Page/CORBIS, *(b)* ©David Ake/AFP-Popperfoto; **p87** *(tl)* ©AFP/CORBIS, *(main)* Associated Press; **p89** ©Tim Page/CORBIS; **p90** *(l)* ©DigitalVision, *(t)* ©Bettmann/CORBIS, *(b)* ©DigitalVision, *(r)* ©DigitalVision; **p91** *(main)* ©DigitalVision, *(tr)* ©CORBIS, *(br)* ©DigitalVision; **p92** *(tl)* ©Bettmann/CORBIS, *(b)* Rex Features; **p93** *(tr)* ©Reuters Newmedia, Inc./CORBIS; **p94** *(l)* ©Hulton-Deutsch Collection/CORBIS, *(b)* ©Peter Turnley/CORBIS, *(tr)* ©Bettmann/CORBIS; **p95** *(mt)* ©Peter Turnley/CORBIS; **p96** *(bl)* ©Bettmann/CORBIS, *(mt)* ©Disney Enterprises, Inc./supplied by Vin Mag Archive Ltd.; **p97** Copyright ©1998, New Line Productions, Inc./The Moviestore Collection; **p98** *(main)* ©DigitalVision, *(l)* ©DigitalVision; **p99** *(tl)* NASA/Science Photo Library, *(tr)* ©DigitalVision, *(br)* ©DigitalVision; **p100** *(bl)* Photo courtesy of STMicroelectronics, *(br)* **www.nhm.ac.uk/museum/index.html** ©The Natural History Museum, London, *(mr)* **www.ancientegypt.co.uk/life/explore/main.html** Copyright ©The British Museum; **p101** *(ml)* **www.childrensmuseum.org/artsworkshop/puppetshow.html** Courtesy of The Children's Museum of Indianapolis, *(m)* "A Gutsy View" graphic image from Human Anatomy Online (**www.innerbody.com**) ©INTELLIMED International Corporation, *(mr)* **weather.yahoo.com/graphics/temperature/Europe_Hi.html** Reproduced with permission of Yahoo! Inc. ©2000 by Yahoo! Inc. YAHOO! and the YAHOO! logo are trademarks of Yahoo! Inc./Map courtesy of Weathernews Inc., the world's largest commercial weather forecasting organization, *(tr)* ©DigitalVision, *(mb)* ©Disney Enterprises, Inc./Ronald Grant Archive, *(br)* ©DigitalVision; **p102** ©AFP/CORBIS; **p103** *(tl)* Alfred Pasieka/Science Photo Library, *(main)* ©Reuters Newmedia, Inc./CORBIS; **p104** Illustrated London News; **p106** ©DigitalVision; **p107** Illustrated London News; **endpapers** ©DigitalVision.